DIARY OF A CI⌐ _____

by Pastor Iuventus

Edited by

DOMINIC ALLAIN

THE CATHOLIC HERALD

GRACEWING

First published in 2008 by
Family Publications and
The Catholic Herald

This edition 2017
by
Gracewing
2 Southern Avenue
Leominster
Herefordshire HR6 0QF
United Kingdom
www.gracewing.co.uk

and
The Catholic Herald
Herald House
15 Lamb's Passage
Bunhill Row
London EC1Y 8TQ
www.catholicherald.co.uk

ISBN 978 0 85244 923 3

FOREWORD TO THE
SECOND EDITION

Pastor Iuventus may no longer be as young as his pseudonym suggests, but as each year passes his writing gains new depth. He is no longer a wet-behind-the-ears priest, struggling to serve Catholics in a single parish. His ministry is now global. He is constantly on the move: leading a retreat for the emotionally wounded here, celebrating Mass for Mother Teresa's Sisters there, counselling seminarians still elsewhere. His column is a kind of travelogue that sheds light on the Catholic Church not only in Britain but also in continental Europe and the wider English-speaking world. What he sees is sometimes disturbing but never, ultimately, without hope. He is an expert at distinguishing between true piety and the kind of religion that is really a subtle form of self-seeking.

One of the most beautiful recent developments is his intense engagement with the Martin family, which famously produced St Thérèse of Lisieux but also several less spectacular examples of holiness. In this family he sees models for Catholics of varied temperaments and abilities.

The theme that connects all his work is vocation. In these pages you will find him wrestling with his own calling, but also helping others to see that God has great plans for them, however weak or insignificant they may feel. His faith enables him to plunge into the darkness and lead others to the light.

Many writers are able to touch either the heart or the head. As you will see in this new edition, Pastor Iuventus is one of those rarities who is able to touch both.

Luke Coppen
Editor of the Catholic Herald
Feast of St Luke, 2017

*This book is dedicated to
James Francis Cardinal Stafford,
at whose hands I was ordained,
and by whose wisdom and example
I am encouraged and inspired.*

FOREWORD

This book presents a selection from what is, for me, the only really indispensable weekly column in the English Catholic press. Shortly after I introduced it in *The Catholic Herald*, I became aware of a real response from our readers, overwhelmingly though not at first universally favourable: it was clear that here was a young priest who believed in and devoutly practised a traditional Catholic spirituality, not to the liking of some who espoused what one of them all too predictably called 'the spirit of Vatican II'; a handful of readers – from widely scattered parishes all over the country – demanded that I confirm their own idea of the identity of 'Pastor Iuventus': they were all convinced that it was their own curate, and wished to complain about him to their bishop.

But it was clear to me that Father Dominic Allain (after a time it became no longer feasible to preserve his anonymity) represented the future, not the past: this was the way the Church, both then under Pope John Paul and now under Pope Benedict, was going and the way most of my readers wanted it to go. They wanted a Church which would nurture a living spiritual tradition, one which would both challenge the spirit of the age and nurture their own spiritual lives.

For most Catholics, the Church is represented by two people: the Pope and their own priest (the diocese and the province tend in their minds to be remote and sometimes bureaucratic entities). Their ideas about the Pope are clear enough: he is regularly reported in the Catholic and the secular media; they can read his encyclicals and hear of his activities. But what is the life of their priest? They see something of it on Sunday in church. But of the daily life of the priest, the life which gives a concrete functioning reality to the parish of which they are part, they have little idea.

Father Allain's column gives them an often vivid inside track on the spiritual life of a parish priest, in a way which certainly conveys its pressures and difficulties, but which also nurtures the spiritual imagination of its readers by demonstrating that those pressures and difficulties can always – with a simple and basic faith in the realities of a working Catholic spirituality – be withstood and transcended. In this, the tenor of his column is very different from that of the Georges Bernanos novel, *Journal d'un Curé de Campagne* (*Diary of a Country Priest*) of which Father Allain's title, *Diary of a City Priest*, reminds us. In one way, the message is the same as that of Bernanos' memorable opening: 'Ma paroisse est une paroisse comme les autres. Toutes les paroisses se ressemblent': 'My parish is a parish like any other. All parishes are like one another.' But Bernanos goes on: 'Ma paroisse est dévorée par l'ennui, voilà le mot. Comme tant d'autres paroisses! L'ennui les dévore sous nos yeux et nous n'y pouvons rien': 'My parish is devoured by apathy, that's the only word for it. Like so many other parishes. Apathy eats them up before our eyes and we can do nothing about it.' The novel in the end is a tragedy, in the end an inspiring one, though certainly not about the possibilities of parish life. One critic described it as 'a deeply moving picture of the triumph of faith over worldly suffering and the worst in human nature.'

No such gloomy rigours await the readers of Pastor Iuventus (which is often very funny about the accidents of parish life) though his column certainly conveys the possibility of a quietly triumphant faith. It is also about the endless fascinations of parish life: there is no apathy here. The message is clear: the life of the ordinary parish, above all through its liturgy, is the gateway to eternity. Here is part of one of Fr Allain's entries for January (the columns are arranged to cover an entire year in the life of the parish):

> On Friday I attended Mass and the consecration of a new altar at one of the churches in the deanery. It was a very moving ceremony in which the altar is treated as a person, for it represents Christ. It is liberally anointed, the bishop literally rolling up his sleeves to spread the oil of Chrism all over the altar. Then incense is burnt on it.
>
> Finally, it is dressed and adorned. Seeing it treated thus, I suddenly realised in a more profound way why we speak of Christ as the priest, the altar and the victim. The priest and the victim are obvious enough, but it is possible to downplay the fact that Christ's human body is the altar;

the place of encounter between earthly man and the all-powerful, holy God.

Always, the message is that we are living between two worlds; the world of earthly sense and secular values in which perforce we must live: and the life of the spirit, a life lived *sub specie aeternitatis*, in the context of eternity: and that we Catholics must live in the world but also be set apart from it: we are called, in Pope John Paul's memorable phrase, to be 'signs of contradiction'. This can lead him to protest against the marginalisation of the Church by the world: a patient in hospital has not been visited by a priest because the chaplains are no longer informed about Catholic patients; the patient's wife is cross, and so is Father Allain; 'There should be far greater lobbying by the Church against this ridiculous application of the privacy laws; they are another way of squeezing faith out of our culture.' Father Allain has a unique gift of being able to understand and reflect the irritations of his people without descending to the merely polemical. But he understands, too, the spiritual importance of taking those irritations seriously: and when they reflect a sense that the Church collectively has let the people down, he is not afraid to say so. As this volume went to press, Pastor Iuventus memorably reflected in *The Catholic Herald* upon the decision last year to transfer holydays of obligation like the Ascension and Corpus Christi to the nearest Sunday:

> In these days of vigil Masses and evening Masses, it can never have been easier to attend Mass on a Holy Day. If people were not attending, the problem is scarcely resolved by moving the feasts to a Sunday, for as we know the percentage of those who see the Sunday obligation as always binding is ever decreasing. For the sake of those who do make the effort to attend, *and as a reminder that the obligation to worship is imposed on us by God himself and is not subject to our convenience*, it is my opinion that this universally unpopular change should be reversed forthwith. [My italics]

Father Allain's may be a column about the spiritual life; but there is never anything mealymouthed about it; always, he writes about the practical circumstances of the spiritual life and how they may be transcended; always, too, we have the sense that the life of eternity is very close and that we may ourselves touch it and appropriate it at any time, as he himself so often and so memorably does. After witnessing a terrible road accident, he prays over a dying man, a vagrant, and absolves him as the ambulance arrives: afterwards, he tells us, 'I walked back to my car. I felt quite wobbly and shaken by the whole thing and filled by a kind of awe. I sat there for a while to recover and then slowly started for home.' Then he reflects:

> Who could tell what the life of that unfortunate man had been? ... God knows; and God knew that this priest was passing today on his way from the printers and could give him the Apostolic Pardon. What are the probabilities of two such random events occurring? Amidst this terrible tragedy was the Providence of God, the ministry of the Guardian Angels mysteriously present.

Always, Father Allain conveys this sense of the closeness of the Providence of God to every human life, no matter how humdrum or how far beyond the margins of human society; and to be able so convincingly to convey the tangible and day-by-day reality of what Carlyle called 'the Immensities' is a rare and precious gift; in *Diary of a City Priest* we see it in action, day by day, week by week, month by month.

Dr William Oddie

8

January

Casualty

I had been to the printers to pick up some parish stationery. It was a nice run, the print works are situated in a pretty little town about fifteen miles outside the city. I must confess I was lingering as long as I could over the trip. I had a cup of coffee in a little Olde Tea Shoppe and a look in some of the bookshops. I was enjoying the drive back relishing the scenery and the break from routine. I was sailing along the dual carriageway when the traffic began to slow; there were flashing lights and all the signs of an accident. I slowed and could see someone lying on the road. There was an ambulance there and a few bystanders; a large tipper truck and a few cars were parked on the hard shoulder.

Now in these situations I never really know what my duty is. Somehow we never talked about it in pastoral classes at the seminary. From priests here and there I have some idea that one should stop. I remember a priest who kept the oil of the sick in his car for such emergencies and another talking about giving someone absolution at the roadside.

I knew I had to stop. I must admit I was anxious, frightened both of what I might find, and what the reaction to my presence would be. Perhaps I would be regarded as a meddlesome intruder. There was a man lying in the road. The first thing I saw was the grizzly sight of a limb some distance away which turned out to be his artificial leg. An ambulance man was bending over him trying to get some response from him. He was deeply unconscious; there was blood all over the road coming from a ridiculously neat wound in his forehead. A bystander was repeating incredulously, "He just stepped out in front of the truck."

The ambulance man greeted me without surprise or hesitation. "Do you know who he is?" he asked. The man was shabbily dressed with a rough beard and looked as if he were a vagrant. I told him I didn't know, that I was just passing. "It doesn't look very good," he said, shaking his head.

Bending low over the man I whispered to him to tell God he was sorry for his sins and I said the words of the Apostolic

Pardon, "By the authority which the Apostolic See has given me, I grant you a full pardon and remission of all your sins." I made the sign of the cross over him and said a Hail Mary. Having done that I prayed silently and held his limp hand till they put him into the ambulance. I think by then he had gone. I wondered whether I should have gone to hospital with him, but felt that it wasn't really my place. Now afterwards I wonder.

I walked back to my car. I felt quite wobbly and shaken by the whole thing and filled with a kind of awe. I sat there for a while to recover and then slowly started for home.

Who could tell what the life of that unfortunate man had been? What was the story behind the false limb and the vagrant life that had ended so cruelly and suddenly by a roadside? Would there be anyone to mourn him save those few frightened good Samaritans who had stopped by the road? God knows; and God knew that this priest was passing today on his way from the printers and could give him the Apostolic Pardon. What are the probabilities of two such random events concurring? Amidst this terrible tragedy was the Providence of God, the ministry of the Guardian Angels mysteriously present.

The scene stayed with me with intensity for the rest of that day and the next. Now it begins to fade somewhat. I am haunted not so much by the distressing scene – the blood and so forth – but the sense of the lonely situation of the victim.

I am left thinking so much about whether the poor man had just wandered into the road or whether he had intended to kill himself. But what counsellors would call "trauma" I also take to be something which connects me with this unknown man at whose dying I had been present. I am conscious that I must pray for him and will say Mass for him when I can. I am conscious too that I was a very small part in something very much bigger, the divine economy of salvation.

And I blessed God who sees even the fall of a sparrow for this mysterious and wonderful vocation he has given me, even though sometimes I feel so totally inadequate and unworthy of it.

A tacky farewell to this life

I am to conduct a funeral at the local crematorium and pass the time of day with the attendant as we wait for the family to arrive. He tells me gloomily that business is slack. This has prompted them to canvass the opinions of their "patrons", by which I presume he means the mourners and officiating clergypersons, to find out why this is – obsequies being one of the few service industries with an entirely dependable market.

It seems that the dramatic nature of the proceedings at this particular crematorium is putting the punters off. I have had reason to comment on it before, for when I first witnessed it I must confess that I was taken aback. For the coffin is placed on a huge canopied catafalque which looks like Nelson's tomb, but in polished oak. At the touch of the committal button the whole shebang descends slowly into the floor, unless you press the button too timidly, in which cases, I am told, the coffin has been known to go down halfway and come up again. It is apparently this descent which is causing people to take their custom elsewhere; the feeling is being expressed that the process is too "final", depending of course, on how you push the button. So the opinion of visiting clergy is being sought as to the desirability of installing a set of optional curtains to surround the catafalque. I am all for it, I tell the attendant, racked instantly with irreverent thoughts of "Hammer House of Horror to Sale of the Century in one easy step".

Actually if the big disadvantage of having so "final" a method of committal is there are fewer such funerals, I am in favour. At least here there is not the usual log jam of hearses at this crematorium as at others. Some crematoria have taken to installing traffic lights – I'm not making this up – to control the flow of funerals.

I don't mean to be offensive, it is just that the application of so impersonal and tacky a method to the disposal of the human body seems profoundly undignified. The atmosphere of such places is always going to be artificial, it seems to me,

12

precisely because they are an attempt to avoid the finality of death. Death is not a passing beyond the curtain; it is a return to dust and ashes. To bury a body in earth is to remind us of our earthiness, our place in creation and the vastness of that creation compared to the littleness of our lives. It is in some way to yield to the body's corruption as one must accept that autumn yields to winter. To whirr some velvet curtains round it is a reminder of cinemas, hotel lounges and only that which is superficial in the human condition. It is not the plush who shall inherit the earth. In the meantime, I mourn the final passing of the catafalque, which seems to me a kind of grand folly, a monument to the tasteless artificiality of the crematorium and therefore of rarity value.

On Friday I attended Mass and the consecration of a new altar at one of the churches in the deanery. It was a very moving ceremony in which the altar is treated as a person, for it represents Christ. It is liberally anointed, the bishop literally rolling up his sleeves to spread the oil of Chrism all over the altar. Then incense is burnt on it.

Finally, it is dressed and adorned. Seeing it treated thus, I suddenly realised in a more profound way why we speak of Christ as the priest, the altar and the victim. The priest and the victim are obvious enough, but it is possible to downplay the fact that Christ's human body is the altar; the place of encounter, the nexus between earthly man and the all-powerful, holy God.

I was also reminded, in the way that a scent alone compels, of my ordination and the scent of Chrism on my hands. The scent is of a deep sweetness that is unlike any sort of cosmetic perfume, but seems to sing of all that is beautiful and in the heart of the earth and of creation – a scent which is like the balm of a medicine but without any astringency, and which is richly perfumed but without any hint of voluptuousness. It is the scent of holiness because it has no other function, no other association than that of consecrating, in the same way as Gregorian chant is the music of holiness because it has no other context, no other association or purpose but the praise of God. The essence of holiness is that something is set apart for God. Because Christ became a man, this setting apart is no longer a kind of gnosticism or dualism – the mistrust of what is earthly – but the highest expression of human life.

For all that is human was set apart for God on the altar of the Cross and henceforth our human nature thirsts for the life hidden with Christ in God which it receives only at his altar.

We belong to God, not to hospitals

The huge ferry slides out of the harbour on a beautiful clear evening, and I reflect that it is a nice way to end a holiday. The coast of Normandy gradually looks smaller and smaller, until the horizon hides it, and after a wistful few minutes watching the churning wake of the boat drifting back towards what has been, it is time to turn your face forward and look for another coast ahead. The end of holidays are much the same, psychologically, I think; there is a time when you look fondly back, and then you turn your face to what lies ahead.

I am delighted to see my parishioners again. Having wandered quite far and wide, I find a real contentment celebrating Mass once again at home, reflecting how beautiful and well cared for the church looks, how lucky we are to have such lovely music and a dignified and prayerful atmosphere to our liturgy, with no nonsense. It is less of a thrill, I must admit, to switch on the hospital pager again. It has been good to be free of that responsibility.

Nor do I have to wait very long for it to start going off again. I have the curious experience of being summoned to a very sick man and when I arrive being told by his relatives that they have changed their minds, and that my presence will distress him too much, alerting him to the danger he is in. I point out the possible alternative, that given he is in such danger my visit, or more particularly the Sacrament of the Sick, might actually be of some comfort to him, but they themselves, who tell me they are not Catholics, remain unconvinced.

I have barely stepped down the ward from this experience when a woman stops me and asks why I have not visited her husband. Because you have neither asked for a visit nor informed the chaplain that the man is a Catholic is the answer. "I naturally thought that as the Catholic chaplain you would visit the Catholics," the woman replies, aggrieved. I have to go in to my explanation that I cannot find out from the hospital Trust who the Catholic patients are because that is a breach of their privacy and therefore their human rights. "But we told them it. It was definitely written on his form when he came in," she protests, not unreasonably. I have to explain further that though it is his human right to manifest his religion on his form and the hospital is supposed to record it, having dutifully recorded the fact that her husband is a Catholic they will tell no one about it. Lewis Carroll would have been proud of such so-called rights legislation. The irate woman's response is the normal, reasonable one: the hospital staff know he is a Catholic; why on earth would they go to the bother of asking for this information and writing it on his form in order not to pass it on to the Catholic chaplain? Why indeed? It's like insisting on asking him if he is a diabetic and then making sure that no one tells the doctors. It only makes sense if you are no longer an individual, somehow, but the property of the health service once you pass through the doors. These "rights" mean, in effect, that they control access to you. In the case of both men they have enshrined as a de facto principle the presumption that the patient would not wish to see a priest.

There should be far greater lobbying by the Church against this ridiculous application of the privacy laws; they are another way of squeezing faith out of our culture. Meanwhile, we need to emphasise again and again the need to tell the chaplain or your parish priest when someone is hospitalised. I wonder what would happen if we tried to introduce some sort of external sign for those people going into hospital. In practice, of course, already one sees a patient with a rosary or a holy picture and realises they are almost certainly Catholic. Perhaps it is time to adopt some official symbol – even a badge of some kind that could be distributed throughout parishes, so that a priest or lay person just walking the wards, could realise quickly who the Catholics were. I wonder how soon it would fall foul of our "rights" legislation.

Oh dear, I am sounding cynical for one so recently returned from holiday, but I have long been suspicious of the rights culture. Positivist rights seem to me all too often to cut great swathes through natural rights. The conception that the state or one of its organs enshrines or codifies your rights automatically gives to the individual the status of client and the state the role of provider and arbiter of rights. No man truly believes he is free because someone who could imprison him keeps telling him it is so. I feel the same about our contemporary culture of rights which gives with one hand and takes away with the other.

Qui Laetificat Inventutem Meam

Only connect, the man said, obviously not thinking of a day retreat for Year Eleven. For the benefit of those who left school before Grange Hill went voluntary-aided and a curriculum was something you had "delivered," Year Eleven is not half as innocuous as it sounds. Year Eleven means, in fact, 16 year olds.

There was a time, I think, when I would have been quite anxious at the prospect of trying to talk to such a group. Perhaps I made the mistake of trying to second-guess what their attitude would be, and forgot that the only person who can get into the head of a 16 year old is a 16 year old. However, I am fairly sure that for most of them a day's retreat at Our Lady's shrine is not high on their list of things to do. Still, the Holy Spirit can work on a residual curiosity or the pragmatist's view that it probably beats a day in school.

Trying to emphasise this positive note, I begin by asking what they would normally be doing in school at this time, reckoning that if they say something hideous like physics or geography I can point out that retreats have a silver lining. "What would you normally be doing in school at this time on a Monday?" I ask only to be met with the sullen answer "break."

Does this throw me? Not a whit. I have prepared well. I prayed hard for them yesterday and I have taken pains with my talks. The Holy Spirit will do the rest. Someone will learn something from it, if only me. I think we can be defeatist and imagine that we have lost before we have begun with young people but I don't believe human nature has changed and human nature needs to hear the gospel loud and clear. It is Good News for human nature. I don't have to apologise for Jesus Christ, I have to make him present.

Nor do I entirely subscribe to the idea that somehow the Christianity product itself is okay but it needs to be repackaged and marketed in a suitably trendy and hip way. The kinds of things that make us think we have to apologise for religion, like an insistence on truth as the value of worth and on ethical standards, are not actually religious virtues. They are in fact human virtues; the kind of thing that at one time marked you out not as a believer, but as a human being capable of using your intelligence to reflect on the nature of the world and the nature of man.

Conversely, the celebrated idealism of young people need not necessarily have anything to do with the gospel, which is addressed to those incapable of making a beautiful world and asks them to repent and allow it to be lovingly made for them, beginning in the waste places of their own hearts. Unless we can persuade young people to save themselves by welcoming Jesus, then all the rainforests in the world will profit them and humanity nought.

I give talks in the morning on Faith and Reason and the Sacraments. Then we have a question box. The boys are invited to write their questions on pieces of paper and I undertake to answer them. A high proportion are concerned with the Church's teaching on sexuality, but that surely is more healthy and more to be expected than questions asking about how many acolytes you field for Pontifical High Mass at the Throne. After all these are the questions that are beginning to exercise their minds and it is positive that they want to know what the Church teaches and why.

There are a lot of questions about evil, about the Devil and about innocent suffering. Good questions; difficult ones. As always with young people there are questions about Hell and about unforgivable sins, as they try to construct a casuistry of mercy. "If I were to do X, but then accidentally forgot to confess it and was killed on my way home from confession, would I go to Hell?" is the kind of thing you will always find youngsters ask.

Then, bless their hearts, they do go to confession. That's a great credit to their families and teachers. They were good confessions too; the toughest and most troublesome among the group suddenly profiled in the beauty of humility.

Lunch and football and then a lovely Mass. I preach and they really are very patient with me. Then the day is over, and I reflect that I may well never see these young people again, for the school is far from the parish and though I get asked there from time to time, next time may well be a different group. But here, today, I ministered Christ to them, not because I understand them or have a gift with young people, I think, but because he can use anyone and has chosen to be present through the ministry of the Church and the priesthood. That is a connection which today might have changed one of these lives forever.

February

Quality of life

He came into the sacristy after Mass and I could tell that something was wrong. He looked as if he was about to cry. Someone had told me that morning that Grace Tate was unwell in hospital but it was one of those occasions when they assume you have been here as long as they have and so know everyone by name. I guessed that this was her husband. He and his wife come to evening Mass on a Sunday, she much frailer than he and needing his help to get up to Communion.

"Father," he said, "I've got to talk to you; I've been awake all night worrying." He went on to explain that his wife was indeed in hospital. She had been admitted at the weekend with some kind of infection. The doctors had seen her on Friday and said that if she had a urinary infection they would treat it with antibiotics; if it turned out to be a chest infection they would not give her antibiotics as her "quality of life" would not merit it. She had seen no doctor since then – it was by now Monday morning. "I can't let them do that Father, can I?" he asked desperately.

I didn't know the ins and outs of the situation, but one thing was absolutely clear. In his own mind, the husband was being asked to consent to the withholding of antibiotics, a routine enough treatment, on the basis of a doctor's decision about the quality of his wife's life. It was painful to see, since he was so devoted to her. His devotion upheld her dignity and asserted the value and quality of her life. I saw the pain in the man's face as he said, "That's like euthanasia, Father; I can't do that."

One look at his face would have provided a profound meditation on the quality of her life. She was loved and cared for by a devoted husband. Offered a way of laying down this burden of care he saw only a terrible betrayal. I cannot believe the doctor can have really seen either him or his wife.

I told him he should insist that they give his wife antibiotics and that judgements about the quality of her life were not the doctor's to make. I said I would come to the hospital that morning. It was a big teaching hospital some miles away. I marvelled at the devotion of the husband who was making this journey two and three times a day on buses. I had never visited it before and managed to get hopelessly lost among the endless different wings and colour coded corridors. If I had not met Mr Tate as I came out of the lift I might have been wandering for hours.

I asked if he had seen the doctor yet. He had not; the doctor was coming back there at 3pm. He took me to his wife. She lay there breathing oxygen and not really fully conscious. I gave her the Sacrament of the Sick, anointing the backs of the bony hands which gripped the sheet tightly. This is such a beautiful sacrament. The signs are so comforting; the hands on the head and the anointings all make visible the healing the sacrament brings. They are signs of gentleness and compassion; God's love for his children in the busy ward with the busy curtains and the oxygen cylinders. For the husband too, I hope, they were a sign of the power of the risen Jesus coming to share and lighten his burden of care.

He checked that Grace was comfortable, told her that he would be back later and we left. I offered him a lift back and so between us we tried to navigate our way out to where I had parked my car in a side street behind the hospital. It was a case of the blind leading the blind. We got hopelessly lost, so poor were the signs. There was one slightly farcical and potentially scandalous moment when Mr Tate tried to lead me through a door marked "Sexually Transmitted Diseases", but I realised in time and we fled. Eventually we found our way out of the maze of corridors and to the car.

He told me, as we drove back, about their 52 years of marriage, how they both came from the same street in Cork but had met in England quite by chance and how they came to our parish 40 years ago.

He was at Mass and came into the sacristy the next morning. I must confess that I feared the worst. Instead he said joyfully, "She's much better Father, you must have healing hands." I was about to wriggle out of the compliment when I thought better of it. After all, God can use anyone, even me. To have healing hands in more or less dramatic ways is part of what He gave me at ordination. I must not treat that lightly, or imagine that it is some reflection on my abilities.

It was a beautiful thing to say. I hope it is true.

Parable of the washing machine

Last Sunday's Gospel proclaimed: "Blessed are the poor in spirit." It was a weekend of swings and roundabouts for my poverty of spirit. On Saturday evening I went to say Mass for a group of Scouts at what they described as a cabin camp. I had romantic visions of a log cabin, but it proved to be a greyer, prefabricated affair set in an attractive woodland off the beaten track but near enough to hear the distant roar of its traffic. There I celebrated a very still, peaceful Mass with a group of 11 year olds. At the end of Mass one of them came up to me and presented me with a chocolate bar and said thank you. It is the kind of gesture you remember for ever. It seems a shame just to eat it.

I came back to the presbytery to find the kitchen floor covered in water. Over Christmas I had noticed water seeping from under the washing machine. I left it alone for a few days and it seemed to be okay. I put it down to temperament on the part of the washing machine. That was clearly a warning shot, however, since the trickle of water had now changed to a large puddle. It was too late even to bother to worry about it. I mopped up as best I could and went to bed. I was bleeped at six o'clock on Sunday morning and came downstairs somnambulantly to find myself paddling in rather a lot of water. It was also a funny colour. Still, there was no time to do anything. I went to the hospital and I closed the door on it.

I was called to a poor man with a lung infection who was greatly distressed and in pain and who kept trying to get out of bed while I was anointing him. I stepped beyond the curtains and stood at the sink scrubbing up. Chaplains, no less than medical staff, are under the strictest instructions to wash hands between patients to avoid spreading infection. (There was a marvellous demonstration on the induction day. Some sort of trace dye was sprayed on our hands. We were then sent off to wash them and when we came back we had to put them in a box which had an ultraviolet light which showed up any

25

remaining specks of the dye. It was the kind of gadget to buy the Macbeths for Christmas.)

So I am standing inches away from the bed, performing my ritual ablutions. With the volume which people always use when curtains are pulled, as though they somehow retain sound, I heard one member of the family say: "It will be better if we get Fr X [their parish priest] down here, at least Dad will recognise him."

I returned home, and as I opened the front door gave way to a whimsical, childhood hope that perhaps while I was out some kind fairies had come in and cleaned and fixed everything. Funnily enough they hadn't. How often as a priest have I had cause to wish I had done courses on plumbing and electrical maintenance as well as eschatology and pneumatology.

On investigation, I discovered that the drain outside the back door appeared to be blocked. I tried to unblock it with wire and by sticking my immaculately washed hand down it, but to no avail. With mounting suspicion I lifted the nearby manhole cover. It was full to the brim with sewage. Two Masses, another visit to the hospital, a First Communion class, a Confirmation class and a pastoral council meeting later, the man from Dyno-Rod arrived. With an air of grim triumph he took me round all four manholes front and back and showed me they were all full. He tut-tutted and grimaced and pulled on his gloves and soon had cleared the blockage with a high pressure jet. I then began the task of trying to wipe and disinfect the kitchen floor, thinking all the while that there must be here some extended metaphor for sin that I could work into a sermon full of powerful counsels always to confront minor difficulties before they become major ones. It didn't come to anything in the end. Then I spent ages washing my hands for the umpteenth time that day, and wondering if all the perfumes of Arabia would ever sweeten them again.

With the precipitous arrival of Lent this year, I had a note in my diary for Monday morning "Remember – order ash for Ash Wednesday!" I know you can make your own, but like homemade cake it's never the same as the stuff you buy in the shops. So first thing Monday morning I phone the long-established church suppliers. The saleswoman tells me ruefully that they can no longer send ash through the post. Apparently last year they caused a major security alert at Mount Pleasant sorting office. The bomb squad thought that half the Catholic churches in England were being sent semtex for the beginning of Lent. You don't know whether to laugh or to cry.

The state gets a foot in the door

A couple of laminated No Smoking signs arrive in the post and a copy of the NHS leaflet entitled Smokefree England (sic). They have been sent, surprisingly enough, not from a government agency, but by the diocesan centre for religious education. In an attempt to give the benefit of the doubt to these good people I thought: "Of course, they are thinking reasonably enough of the church hall, or the presbytery." But no, the information quite clearly stipulates that No Smoking signs must be displayed in church. This is a total absurdity, since no one has ever smoked in a church unless they were mad, and mad people are not going to pay much heed to No Smoking signs. That clearly counts for nothing in our brave new world.

The Stalinist tone of the NHS leaflet sends shivers down my spine. Under the question "Why is this (the displaying of No Smoking signs) necessary?" it explains that the signs "will demonstrate that the church authorities are taking the necessary steps to meet the requirements of the new law. They also provide some degree of legal protection in the unlikely event of someone being caught smoking on church premises."

That is a staggering statement. It effectively admits that the signs are not necessary, since someone lighting up in church is an unlikely event and, moreover, by putting a sign up such an unlikely event can just as easily occur. So the answer to the question "why is it necessary?" comes back: because this law says so, to show that churches will jump through unnecessary legislative hoops. The sign becomes significant only when you fail to display it. It is only important because if someone smokes in your church and you haven't put up a sign you can be punished. Any regulation thus ill-conceived, arbitrary and lacking in common sense must have a threat behind it in order for it to be complied with. That much is nothing to do with public health, it's about state proscription. "You must have a sign because we say so and the consequences to good order or public health that will follow from your not having a sign are that you will be punished for the offence of not having a sign." Legislation is now master not servant of public good, and at issue is something deadly serious – the right to police what happens in churches.

The language used in the leaflet leaves you in no doubt about this. It suggests that if you have any doubts as to where to put such a sign (don't go there ...) you speak to your local environmental health officer who will be responsible for "compliance".

"It is not the intention of enforcement authorities to approach churches in a punitive way," says the leaflet. How very big-hearted of the "enforcement authorities". A law so necessary, so positive for public health and so manifestly just that "enforcement authorities" will police its compliance with a rigour which will depend on their leniency has a very un-English ring to it. The English have traditionally been the most law-abiding people in the world because our conception of Common Law means that responsible subjects have an interest in the keeping of the law which is seen to impose as little possible on people's lives, providing they are doing nothing dangerous or harmful, and bound all equally with the duty to uphold it. The implications of this legislation should frighten everyone regardless of what they think about smoking. This is about whether you can break the law by not telling someone not to do something they haven't yet done. This is an issue about control, about the ability of the state to legislate people's behaviour in every sphere and place. (One of my parishioners who lives in a housing association property has heard from her local authority health officers that under the new legislation she is "permitted" to smoke in her own home. It demonstrates the same frightening conception that the state is the arbiter of freedom.)

I have never smoked. As a mild asthmatic I loathe smoking and smoky atmospheres. I agree that employees and the public should not be exposed to what the document calls "second-hand smoke". Now, a whole army of state-funded compliance officers will be empowered to come and check whether there are No Smoking signs displayed in churches. These are two entirely different aims.

If we accept that freedom now depends on the beneficence of enforcement authorities, and no longer requires that the law should be proportionate, commonsensical and respectful of corporate personalities like church communities, then this legislation has implications for absolutely everything that goes on in church. In terms of how they affect churches as "public places", the provisions of this law derive not from public health, moral authority or justice but from the power of the state to dictate to people. If you think that sounds extreme, ask yourself why the one public place where this law will not apply is the Houses of Parliament and the Palace of Westminster.

Garden of the Soul

Asked to do a Shrove Tuesday recollection for a nearby prep-school, I decide to use Oscar Wilde's beautiful story 'The Selfish Giant' to get the children thinking about what sin is, what sin does.

The powerful imagery of the garden behind the high walls where it is always winter and never spring speaks to me strongly of the human heart and sin. Despite the giant's selfishness, the children slip into the garden, including one unknown child who is too small to climb a tree. The giant lifts him into a tree and as he does the tree breaks into blossom.

He does not see the child again for years, until one morning, in the depths of winter he sees a corner of the garden in blossom, and the child standing there, now with the prints of two nails on his hands, and the prints of two nails on his feet.

"These are the wounds of Love," says the child, in answer to the giant's anger on seeing them. "You let me play in your garden; today you shall play in my garden which is paradise."

The children are spellbound by the story. When it is finished, I ask them what the word Lent means. They give many intelligent answers: "A period of forty days," "A time of fasting," "Time for giving something up." Then I tell them that it is the Old English word for Spring. Put in this way I hope it becomes something more positive, and with the help of the story's powerful imagery I try to develop the idea of Lent as a time when we look for new growth, for springtime in our hearts by dying a little to selfishness.

This is followed by confessions; the good, transparent confessions of children whose words ring like crystal, delicate and true. They have not yet learnt to see sin as a reason for hiding from God. We finish with Benediction. I have the usual moment of anxiety when giving Benediction in a strange place. Is there some fiendish knack to opening the tabernacle; is there some intricate fastening for fitting the lunette and host into the monstrance? Fortunately things are reasonably straightforward and the Benediction is prayerful and dignified.

And so to Ash Wednesday. The ash arrived last week from the Church requisites supplier. I had phoned a couple of weeks ago to see about ashes and palms and got a very helpful lady who looked at her computer screen and told me that we have a standing order for ash and palms. I had no idea that the world of palms and ash had become so high-tech.

All credit to her, the ash duly arrived a couple of days later, in small, sealed polythene packets of the sort you see in police dramas. I half-expected someone to dip his finger into one and put some ash on his tongue to see if it was genuine.

I say the morning Mass and then hurry to the school for their Mass. I try my question on the meaning of the word Lent on the children here too, with similar results. There is always something particularly poignant about marking children with ashes and saying "Remember man that thou art dust and unto dust thou shalt return."

The problem, it seems to me, is that it is easy not to remember; to imagine that I am a self-starter when it comes to God, that I can choose to favour him with my attention as and when it suits me. I forget that if he were for a moment to cease to think of me or love me I would relapse into non-existence. I do not remember that I am creature, wholly dependent on him, and that if I am to be happy I need to play things his way. It is his world, his creation, and he has made me knowing what best will conduce to my happiness.

It is impossible to mark a couple of hundred foreheads of all ages and conditions with ash and not find yourself reflecting Hamlet-like on what a piece of work is man.

I have in my breviary a photograph of a statue from Chartres Cathedral of God creating Adam. God is moulding a face out of the clay which mirrors his own. This is the truth, that though we are made of dust God was prepared to expend first of all a universe of creation and then his own Son on man to redeem him and set us on the throne of heaven.

In Lent I need to embrace my dependence, my nothingness.

Into this he can breathe his Spirit anew. The English Metaphysical poet Thomas Traherne writes:

In thy word Lord is my trust
To thy mercies fast I fly
Though I am but clay and dust
Yet thy grace can lift me high.

March

The great springtime of the faith

Glorious spring weather allows me to spend a few hours hacking things down in the garden. I have been pruning viciously so as to ensure not just new growth, but some sort of respectable shape to several rather unruly trees and shrubs which I inherited, and also a greater opportunity for the sunlight to get to some corners of the garden which seem to be in shadow all the time. Lent, of course, is the Anglo-Saxon word for springtime, so metaphors of gardens for passions rather force themselves on one. I trust my Lenten pruning speaks for itself.

The glorious spring weather prompts not just plants but people to sudden spurts of activity. At my "surgery" on Monday evening I had three couples coming to inquire about getting married (at one point we had people queueing four-deep in the office). Of the three, none wants to marry here. That has been my experience thus far: there are still a relatively high number of people coming to inquire about weddings, all of whom are going elsewhere for the ceremony itself — most to Ireland.

It becomes mildly dispiriting to feel that you are just running a sort of marriage preparation bureau, processing the papers and preparing the couple, only to wave them off for a lovely ceremony somewhere else. I know: I should be pleased that they are marrying, and of course I am, but it's hard not to feel whatever the clerical equivalent of "always the bridesmaid, never the bride" is, especially when faced with a "hat trick" in one evening.

It is more than slightly frightening to think that Lent is half over. It seems a shame that this induces a slightly frantic feeling — not so much of living for the acceptable time, but of constantly thinking ahead to the celebration of Holy Week and trying to make sure everything is ready. This week, I must get to grips with the music so that the choir has a chance to practise it and we can put together booklets for the congregation. It is desirable to have some kind of customised service sheets for the Holy Week ceremonies, otherwise you seem to spend half the time giving out instructions and liturgical vade mecums. The palms are on a standing order; the paschal candle is selected; from a logistical point of view all is ready. However, the electricians are due in this week to overhaul the sanctuary lighting, so, as the song says, there may be trouble ahead.

The local branch of the Guild of Catholic Doctors held its annual Lenten recollection at the weekend. I thought they had probably tired of listening to me, and so I was emboldened to invite a very eminent theologian who has recently moved to the area. He taught for years at the Jesuit university in Rome and has retired from there but still has a busy programme of lectures and talks and writing on the go. I was a student of his, and knew of his exceptional gift for making his theological expertise not only accessible to all, but of service to a vivid, Spirit-filled preaching of the Gospel. Sure enough, he gave an inspiring recollection on the theme of the beauty of Jesus.

I was delighted that we had so great a "resource", for these Catholic doctors are of some eminence themselves in their field, but also are a shining example of lay people committed to being light and salt in the difficult world of medical practice, and I feel they need every support. On a personal level, it was a great pleasure to see my old professor again and to be able to welcome to part of my pastoral care someone who was so helpful in preparing me for it.

One new aspect of the Lenten journey this year has been accompanying the RCIA group. As one of them prepares for baptism and three for reception into the Church at Easter, their commitment and excitement is wonderful to see.

As so often, while I am concentrating on seeing that they are reasonably calm and prepared, they are teaching me by their demeanour that one never celebrates two Easters the same, that each year the heart should once again be staggered at the mystery of God's love shown us in the dying and rising of Jesus, and the fact that this power is poured out anew on us who participate in its liturgical re-enactment, so that for each of us it can be said to be a new beginning, another wonderful step in our conversion. Actually, they have been a real inspiration to me. One of them announced en passant that he was attending Mass every day in

Lent. Another decided that she wanted to celebrate her First Confession with her children, who were making their own in preparation for their First Holy Communion.

There is joy and wonder at seeing new life abundant in the springtime of the Church's year.

Stations

One evening I visit a couple who are hoping to marry in the winter.
I say hoping to, the would-be-groom is awaiting the annulment
of a previous marriage, or to be more correct, is waiting for
his previous marriage to be declared null. I agree a provisional
date for the wedding, and then wonder if this is kind or wise. I
keep stressing that it is dependent on the outcome of the nullity
process. He assures me that the tribunal say it is "as good as in the
bag." I would be surprised at any tribunal saying that; I think it is
what he wanted to hear. I ask him a bit about the case and on the
face of it, in my inexpert opinion, it sounds as if he should get
the annulment.

In the course of the conversation he mentions to me that he is
so anxious to get married "properly" so that he can begin to receive
Holy Communion again. I tell him that although he is divorced he is
neither remarried nor living with his intended wife and therefore I
can see no reason why he should not receive Communion providing
he has been to Confession. The news overwhelms him and he breaks
down. What a healing this will bring him.

Out visiting the housebound with Holy Communion the next
day and one of my ladies isn't answering her door. I get a bit
worried. I phone her on my mobile, no answer. Then I reflect
that she might just have had a hospital appointment and forgotten
to tell me, but that's not like her. I try calling though the letter
box but there is no answer. I try looking through the windows
into her bedsit, but can see nothing. I think if she had fallen or
something I would probably be able to see her. What should I
do? There could be some perfectly straightforward reason for
this, but I worry that she may be ill inside. I know she has a
daughter in the Midlands but don't have a number to call. The
neighbours are all out, I don't know who else to ask. I see this
lady every week and yet really know very little about her. In
the end I decide that I will leave it. She has carers going in daily
from the social services and they would know if she were ill so
I don't think she has been left helpless. If she is not answering

her phone tomorrow I will perhaps try and find out where she is from social services.

I move on. One of my ladies has gone to Heaven and instead of visiting her this week I shall be celebrating her funeral Mass. She had been suffering from Alzheimer's and it was hard to know how much she understood of what was going on. I think she certainly knew she was receiving Holy Communion; she would become much more animated and tremble as I said, "This is the Lamb of God".

The glorious spring weather continues until Sunday. Suddenly the blossoms are out and the garden needs attending to. I take the hints and get out there on a Sunday afternoon with the lawnmower, but the grass is too long and still too wet to make much headway. There is something energising about being out there in the sunshine, and the smell of new-mown grass fills the house all evening. I reflect how wise St Benedict was when he designed a life that balances work, prayer and study. I don't feel like there's much balance in mine at the moment, at least it feels too full of catching up. All the studying is for tasks, for talks I must finish or sermons I must give and never just for studying, and there's too much sitting at a computer and in a car.

On Sunday evening we have Stations of the Cross, and in a moment of silence during them I hear an unfamiliar sound, bird song and I realise that the evening is still light. I meant to remind the people about putting the clocks on next week; that will catch some of them out. I was distracted when giving the notices by a terrible misprint in the newsletter.

I hate proof-reading, I haven't the patience for it. Stations have been attracting a goodly number, including some of the youngsters, which is excellent. For most of them it is their first time serving Stations and Benediction.

As we return to the sacristy for the second time after Benediction, young William says to me ruefully, "There isn't a part three, is there Father?" I assure him there isn't.

Solving a grave problem

We had a St Patrick's night dance last week in the function suite of a local pub. With nowhere of our own to hold them we have few social functions, so it was a great gathering of the clans and a very enjoyable evening. The place had been decorated with flags and bunting and shamrock motifs. There was a certain amount of consternation when the "band" turned up, for it turned out to be a middle-aged, bearded Hell's Angel minus motor bike, but correct in all other respects, with beard and tattoos and piercings. Here, you said to yourself, is a strange band, the kind that if you asked did it know the Siege of Ennis would probably roll up his sleeves and show you scars. He duly assembled a variety of hardware which seemed to provide him with a sophisticated electronic accompaniment for the guitar or banjo which he would play while singing. He seemed to know which buttons to press – I mean in the sense of selecting the right tunes, a fair mixture of Irish, and sort of country and western, folksy music, what one might call easy listening, though the volume meant that it wasn't that easy. Certainly any conversation had to be carried on in a shout, so that by the following morning I had ringing in the ears and was hoarse.

I have no wish, however, to join the ranks of the begrudgers. Inevitably there were some who said as it was too cheap, some who said as it was too dear, some who felt that the music was not lively enough and others who felt it was too lively, some who would have preferred more food, and some less. What's the good of these things if there are no talking points, after all? At one stage I feared I was going to be drawn into an unpleasant raffle-fixing scandal when I managed to draw winning tickets for two of its organisers and another one for my mother whom they had kindly invited. There's no doubt though that it was a fun evening and a great boost for parish morale. We raised over £1,000 profit towards our hall. So there you are. Just another dance every week for the next five years and we will be able to build it!

I have to say that, for me, one of the best things about the evening was seeing Jack there. He lost his wife about this time last year and they had both been away from the Church for a long time. Since then he has become one of our most regular attenders and is becoming involved in the life of the parish more and more. It was lovely to see him there with his daughter and some friends. It made me realise how, even in trying to build a hall, we are already building a community. I will always remember Jack's wife's funeral vividly because when we got to the committal at the graveside the coffin was too big for the grave. It couldn't be lowered – it stuck in the mouth of the grave. I was told afterwards by another local clergyman that this is a better outcome than lowering it and finding it gets stuck half way down. If it is actually in the grave, even by just a few inches, you apparently need a Home Office permit to take it out: it is technically an exhumation. I am assured also that if a mourner should accidentally drop something into a grave – a handbag, for instance – you cannot simply fish it out again; you require special permission from the Home Office.

To give them their due, the cemetery staff and gravediggers were absolutely mortified at what had happened, the cemetery warden apologising profusely, saying it hadn't happened to him in all the 30 years he had worked there. It seems there was some kind of breakdown in communication between them and the undertakers about what size the coffin was.

What could we do? We had to just stand there and wait while the gravediggers fetched their spades and shaved a few more inches of earth off the foot of the grave, until finally the coffin could be lowered. In the strange, tense moments of waiting I went over to Jack, a great gentle giant of a man, without much idea of what I could say.

"You will tell this story over and over again," I told him, "and in time to come you will perhaps even be able to smile about it."

"I know," he said, with a rueful smile, "I will tell them how she didn't want to leave me."

I have always remembered his dignified bearing in the midst of what had potential either for farce or outrage. I am so happy that he has become part of our community, that he felt he wanted to come and join in the dance.

Taking clubbers to the cloister

The paschal candle and winter arrived yesterday. It is bitterly cold, and the wind whips through the presbytery's double-glazing, which seems to have all the insulating effect of medieval stained glass with none of the concomitant catechetical charm.

I am just back from leading a retreat for a group of sixth formers at a retreat centre attached to a Benedictine monastery. It was an ideal place; the young people are able to experience a taste of the monastic liturgy and the atmosphere of the monastery, but also have a slightly less austere time than they would if we were staying in an enclosure. You can sell it, in part, as an experience of time away with friends. It was a lovely time. There's no doubt that they were impressed by their surroundings, challenged by the monastery, moved by the liturgy and genuinely motivated by the desire to pray. We had several conferences, a "question box" and plenty of time for private and communal prayer. They all participated in a Holy Hour before the Blessed Sacrament and every one of them celebrated the Sacrament of Penance, which is quite remarkable in itself and a sign that they were open to the promptings of the Spirit. We had recreational activities too: a fascinating tour of the incense workshop with the abbot, and a mammoth game of Trivial Pursuit; 17 of us sat on the floor round the board in teams.

All that being so, what I say isn't intended to detract from that, or diminish the impression I have that for many of them it was a very worthwhile experience. But what strikes me, given how good and well-motivated these young people obviously are, is just how much work there remains to be done. Culturally, they are miles away from where they need to be if they are to persevere in their faith. Religion has to prove its claims against the more immediate satisfactions of the consumer age. I thought the comment of one girl as we left Compline spoke volumes: "Not one of them looks as if he has ever been to a club." It was said sympathetically, as if to say, "the poor dears". I don't suppose she would ever go into a club and say, "Not one of them has ever seriously explored the interior life", in the same tone of voice.

It was interesting to see how they coped with something as fundamental as the challenge of silence. At that sort of age silence is not something which necessarily comes easily or naturally. The world meets the cloister in a particularly striking way when you ask them to switch off their mobile phones for a few hours. You can see that some of them are really thrown.

The "question box" session, in which they are invited to ask anything they want, revealed that the idea of the obedience of faith towards the teaching of the Magisterium just doesn't really figure. The crisis is a deep-rooted one; it is the problem of subjectivism, and the idea that any one person's conviction must be as valid as anyone else's. In such an atmosphere, the notion of truths which are universally valid breaks down, long before you start to think of revealed truths. One boy said he thought you could probably never say anything was absolutely true, but he wasn't sure that he wanted to say that definitely, apparently unaware of the torturous syllogism of such a statement. Such an attitude paralyses faith, just as surely the inability to ever trust another person paralyses love.

There is also an almost systematic scepticism towards the claims of the Church. If only our youth applied half as much scepticism to current shibboleths of animal rights, the environment or sexual politics. Again, they seem to start with the view that these are incontrovertibly self-evident. This is not because anything in their experience necessarily bears them out, but because no one can actually live without taking things on authority; for so many people, not just the young, authority now lies with what most people seem to be saying and doing.

In the face of this we need to be like John Paul II and Benedict XVI and find a language which challenges young people to examine what it is they truly are seeking. We also need to proclaim fearlessly that only in encountering Jesus Christ can they become truly themselves. It is, of course, not enough to tell them this. They need the witness of men and women in whom the Gospel has taken root and who have a deep knowledge of the human heart. We need saints who, with infinite patience and love, will enflesh for them that love of God, which beyond their struggles and difficulties and failures sees the dignity and beauty which is theirs and embraces it, loving it into life.

April

Passover

Ten days before Easter and the palms have arrived, a huge bundle wrapped in brown paper. One of our stalwarts will take them down to the hall and painstakingly separate the fronds into individual palms.

Here we preserve the old custom of veiling the statues from the fifth Sunday of Lent, the old Passion Sunday. It is such a dramatic change, it brings an intensity to one's Lenten preparations. The shrouded forms of the statues are disquieting, there is a reminder of death there, something vaguely fearful, but also intriguing – a mysterious outline.

The early part of Holy Week is fairly tranquil, with the schools broken up, and no more recollections or talks to give, just sermons to prepare. The routine business of parish life goes on but the season gives everyday things a new poignancy. While we prepare to celebrate the Paschal mystery with minds and hearts renewed, the mystery of God's saving action is coming to completion in the lives all around. Mass on Sunday is for Len Harman's wife. He booked it just last week for her anniversary; 8 o'clock Sunday morning – he never misses. Len died on Monday. He will be buried with her and rejoicing with her in Heaven by the time we say Mass for his intentions on earth.

I visit the hospital to see a couple of our parishioners. It cannot be said often enough from the pulpit, and in print, that people need to tell their priests when someone is in hospital. The first man I went to see was delighted and surprised. "I didn't think I would see you," he said; "When I asked to see a priest, they said, 'What do you want to see a priest for?'" It is always thus. Rights become duties. Your right to privacy means that hospital chaplains no longer have access to records showing who the Catholics are. I said I would take up the matter with the NHS Trust, but I haven't yet managed to track down who I should contact.

I then spend a convivial few minutes waiting for the lifts. They are so slow and intermittent that a sort of spirit of the

Blitz mentality seems to pervade and perfect strangers strike up friendships. I imagine it's a twenty-first century equivalent of how it was in biblical times as you queued to draw water at the well. All the same, I had quite a bellyful of it by the time I tracked down the patient I was seeking, who had been moved three times, to three different floors. Eventually I found her. She looked very small and frail, seeming to have diminished physically in proportion to her distress at leaving her little home and her life of independence. It was her modesty, as much as her pride, that was suffering from this change.

She is a dear spinster lady in her 90s, a sort of ideal maiden aunt. I have been taking her Holy Communion at home for some time now until this crisis landed her in hospital. She has great faith and the way she spoke confirmed that. On the one hand she spoke with equanimity about her death and discussed her funeral arrangements. On the other hand she spoke of her fear of dying. Would she see her mother and father when she died, she asked, and suddenly she was talking more freely than she ever had. She told me all about her mother and father and about her four brothers whom she loved. She had lived with them, and she had 15 nephews and nieces. "I call them my children," she said, "they are like children to me." She was like a child, full of anxious questions.

"How will I know when God is calling?" she asked. " There is a grace which comes with dying," I said, without really knowing where it came from. "Will I have to spend a long time in Purgatory?" I told her that the suffering of Purgatory was different from the sufferings of Hell, a deeply intense longing; knowing that salvation was assured and that "a long time" was not really about its duration. She was worried that she could not pray; I told her just to hold her rosary and to think of the whole Church praying for her, including her parents and her brothers in Heaven. I promised to say Mass for her on Monday and she asked me to write it down in a little notebook she had with her. She paused and said: "I have no doubts about the faith, but I wouldn't mind a little reassurance."

"Become what you celebrate," says St Augustine, of the Holy Eucharist. As we celebrate the Christian Passover once more, from death to life, from slavery to freedom, we might reflect that it is a celebration that doesn't merely enrich our lives. It is what gives them shape and form. It is their mystery, now veiled and seen in outline, soon to be unveiled in the glory of the resurrection of Our Lord Jesus Christ.

Jesus in the hands of a fragile man

Maundy Thursday began with a call to the deathbed of a dear, sweet lady in her late 80s whom I knew from my previous parish. I can still see her blithely knocking over the picket fence in the car park as she drove her ancient Metro to Mass one day. She seemed frail then, but full of an indomitable will. When I saw her first in the hospital a few days ago, she seemed to have shrunk away physically, as if it was only this will which was keeping the fragile little body going, a bright flame from a shrinking candle. I commended her to Almighty God and thought it rather beautiful that someone who had been so faithful to daily Mass should go to Him on Maundy Thursday.

Fr Shaughnessy was the beloved parish priest of St Gabriel's near here for many, many years and retired about three years ago. I heard he was in hospital so I went to visit him with Holy Communion. I found it very moving to read the Gospel of the Mandatum with him, and give him Holy Communion, this man who had ministered for 55 years and now was graciously allowing himself to be like Peter and ministered to — which, as we know, is not an easy thing to do, for it requires our humility, our being aware of our neediness and essential frailty. I asked his prayers for all I had to do in the next few days. There were times when I wondered whether I could physically cope with it.

From there I went to another hospital: the mental health unit of a satellite of our Trust to see Tommy-Joe. Fortunately it was handy for the dean's house, where I had to pick up the newly blessed Holy Oils. Tommy-Joe is at Mass every week. He is hard to age; he could be 60. Very, very diffident and quietly spoken he comes to the sacristy every once in a while for a bottle of holy water for his elderly mother with whom he lives. She moved into the new house when the council first built the large estate after the war. I visit her every so often with Holy Communion; her bad knees and her catarrh stop her going out. She told me today that Tommy-Joe has had a nervous breakdown and is in hospital. She told me, as she does every time I go, of his previous breakdown. It happened after his father died, for they were very close. She told me the whole sad story and then finished as she always does by sighing: "Still, what can you do? That's life."

When I located Tommy-Joe's ward in the complex of attractive modern units (all apparently named after shades of emulsion: Acacia, Apple Blossom, Azalea, etc.) he was having supper, but I managed to speak to him for a while in a room across the corridor. He was not as bad as I expected, but clearly was very fragile. He had the scared eyes and the jumpiness of a cornered animal about him. Jesus puts himself into his hands in that most unthreatening, most docile sign of the Sacred Host and Tommy-Joe receives him with devotion.

There was little time to pause and think about these encounters; it was time to get home to be ready for the Mass of the Lord's Supper. They came back to me, and many others like them over the past few weeks, as I watched at the altar of repose later on. I realised that all such encounters make for me a kind of mosaic; increasingly they combine in colour and texture with the liturgical part of the celebration of Easter to form a more complete kind of picture. I begin to see that the dying and rising of Jesus is not just something the Church tacks on to our experience of death in the way that an airline tags your luggage at check-in before it disappears into oblivion. The mystery of Christ's dying and rising is with us already through our baptism. We celebrate it not just because it happened once or might have some relevance to our personal future. It is all around us: Christ yesterday and today, the beginning and end of what we tend to think of as a separate reality. Easter faith, in fact, is to see that there is only one reality of existence which is contained by the Paschal Mystery of Jesus Christ. Tommy-Joe's mother had said it already in a tone of complete acceptance – that's life. Life is about dying and rising, about suffering and new life, and now Christ is the Alpha and Omega of all things. Life is hidden with Christ in his dying and his rising.

We should live and love now in the joyful hope that Christ has redeemed sorrow and death in us, for us. The mysteries of suffering and death which seem to take us into non-existence are the mysteries of the extremest reach of God's love, revealed in concealment like the empty tomb of Jesus which proclaims he is not there, he is risen. Where Jesus least seems to be, there he is most.

A cry of life in the Darkness

This year we had a baptism at the Easter Vigil. It seems to reveal the ceremony as something more dynamic even than a dramatic remembrance of the historical fact of the Resurrection.

More than ever, I am conscious that running through the liturgy is the message that not only is Christ risen, but that he is risen for us and that is the start of a new life for all of us baptised into him. This is the night, as the Exultet sings over and over again, when the salvation prefigured in the Passover is visited on us, when a new life becomes our lot.

This new life derives not merely from the recollection of what Christ once did, but is a present power, through the action of Christ in the liturgical celebration, in the living power of the sacraments. One celebrates the Resurrection truly by living it out now, in this life of grace.

This is no mere scene change from Good Friday. The message of the scripture and the tradition is clear – that the Resurrection is a new kind of creation, a new reality.

The Gospel is this proclamation; that the body which died on the cross and laid in the tomb is risen; not resuscitated, but risen to a new kind of reality in which death no longer has any power. God has confronted this evil and drawn its venom.

This is much more of a wonderful thing than Jesus pulling a rabbit out of the hat of suffering.

It means that human nature has a new way of being. This is why we celebrate Sunday as the first day of the week: it is the first day of a new creation.

Rising each day we can say: "This day was made by the Lord." We must begin our week with the encounter with the risen Jesus in Holy Communion. For we live an Easter life. Through baptism, which in its old manner of full-immersion, imitates the action of dying and rising, we already share in the new life of Easter, the life of victory over suffering, the life lived for God. Any life apart from this is meaningless: it remains stalked by the same old fears and difficulties.

Baptism includes us in the infinity of God's love, drawing us upwards from the non-life of our sins, from the littleness of those sins we cling to in order to try to stave off our fear of our weakness, our essential loneliness, our poverty. This is no life at all.

Our true life is hidden with Christ in God. We search for this life in which we are beloved sons and daughters, graced with the love which heals and validates us. It continually raises us up even as our mortal bodies exist in the realm where all things wear out, all things are passing.

The Easter renewal of our baptismal promises cannot be mere ritual, it must be accompanied by a genuine, heartfelt desire to live the new life of grace, the immensity of which outweighs all the things we once thought important. The crisis of death is not what happens to our bodies, it is what happens to our ability to impact on others or be anything to others by our love.

If we have found the true life, hidden with Christ in God, then there is nothing to harm us. Our loving shares in his victory over sin and death, for it will become like his, who for our sake, became as we are. In the words of Gerard Manley Hopkins: "I am all at once what Christ is, for he was what I am and this Jack, joke poor potsherd, patch matchwood immortal diamond, is immortal diamond."

Thank God for the "high" of the Easter Vigil, and for the grace which comes from celebrating the Triduum. For the challenge to live this new life is no easy one. The old life runs its course, challenges our hope. I am woken early on Easter Sunday by a call to baptise a premature baby.

In between Easter Masses I see 17 patients in hospital in various states of illness. Late on Easter Sunday and more tired than I thought it possible to be, I am again called to bless a still-born baby.

The parents do not wish to be present or to see me. I bless the tiny, perfect body all alone in the Easter evening, only not alone, because Christ is risen, and this faith is at once as powerful and as weak as the single candle with which we shatter the darkness and cry "Lumen Christi".

Whose sins you forgive ...

This week I heard twenty or so First Confessions. The sincerity and honesty of children in this sacrament are inspiring. There is no distance, no equivocation, between their examination of conscience and what they tell you.

Their confessions are very concrete; they clearly have specific instances in mind which they recognise as sinful. They will often go into unnecessary details when confessing things like fighting with their brothers and sisters; it is as if they experience very vividly the sense of the wrong done.

Perhaps they are scared the first time round; some catechists and parents play up the idea that children are terrified. I often think that they are projecting something of their own feelings about confession onto their children, trying to exorcise their own ghosts. I am not a parent, but as a priest I can honestly say that it is very rare for children to appear unduly frightened by the sacrament of confession. Some children may well find it difficult; many new experiences can be, but that doesn't mean we can or should avoid them. There are some innocently humorous moments: "Bless me Father, for I have sinned against you", "Oh my God because I am so good . . ." When I raise my right hand to give absolution to one child she assumes she must do the same and there we sit, like Indian chiefs, either side of the grille.

I had an interesting experience on Easter Sunday. I was locking up the church. I felt a tremendous sense of peace, as well as feeling totally exhausted. Very often on Sunday evenings there is a small figure in a neat hat scurrying round the back of the church. It is Sadie. It is her self-appointed task to scurry round the church and pick up all the dropped missalettes and bulletins and then she tidies up the newspapers and the various displays in the porch. She is the sort of person who will never be on a committee or be a catechist or a Special Minister. Her involvement consists of coming faithfully to Mass and staying for her thanksgiving and clearing up the church – she is really precious.

She must have been at one of the morning Masses, I thought. Then I noticed there was someone in church. It was a child, kneeling on the prie-dieu in front of the Lady Altar looking up at the statue.

I hadn't seen him in church before. He was about eight and had closely shaved hair and a dirty face. There was a slightly hard look about his face, but his eyes were wide and bright. My grandmother would have called him a "little urchin"; he was the kind of child you would cast as the Artful Dodger. I waited in the sacristy, so as not to be alone in the church with him, for such is the world in which we must operate. I have to admit I was slightly worried that he might be up to no good. When he left I finished tidying the place up and then left the church full of candlelight and locked the front door.

As I came out of the side door I saw the boy sitting on the porch steps. He got up when he saw me and asked anxiously, "Was it alright for me to come in?" I said he was very welcome and asked him if he had been to church before. "No," he said. "Do your Mum and Dad know you have come?" I asked. "No," he said. "A lady told me I could come, she's called Sadie; do you know her?" I said I did. "Her grandson's my mate. She told me I could come here. Can I do that thing where you say all the 'fings what you've done wrong?"

I questioned him and realised he was asking for confession. I chatted a bit more with him and decided he probably wasn't baptised, let alone a Catholic. Nonetheless, I heard his "confession" there on the steps and we said an Act of Contrition together and I gave him a blessing and sent him on his way, telling him to tell his parents where he had been and to be sure and come again.

I deliberately went back into the church and read John's Gospel telling how it was evening on the first day of the week and the doors were closed for fear of the Jews. Jesus came and stood among them and, breathing on them, gave the apostles the gift of forgiving sins in his name. In that child drawn here on Easter night, was a message from God; that the Easter gift of forgiveness of sins corresponds to the deepest needs of the human spirit. It is the way in which we are changed to receive the life of Jesus risen. It is the sacrament of Easter Evening, in which Jesus comes through the locked doors of our hearts. Children are used to the degree of trust this requires. We adults must re-learn it.

May

Inspired by a people in exile

The weather forecasters were wrong: the bank holiday was a lovely, bright day, though not what you would call warm. Normally bank holidays don't make much difference to my routine, but this Monday, for the first time in a long time, I had a day without any calls to the hospital. I was able to do a bit of gardening and ironing, and even watch a little of Ben-Hur.

On Saturday I went to bless a house. To the Filipino couple who have bought it, it must seem like something of a dream. Though a very modest place on a rather run-down council estate, it is costing them somewhere in the region of 160 times what a house would cost in the Philippines. The house blessing is an integral part of what turns out to be a housewarming party.

When I arrive at 4pm friends and neighbours are there waiting and the party commences with my blessing the house. Then there is a sumptuous feast laid on, provided by family and friends. I know that they are in some ways a community in exile, which always strengthens bonds, but it is impossible not to be moved by the way that family, faith and community all come together in this celebration. What is being celebrated is not just a housewarming, not just a foot on the property ladder; this is a celebration of home, of putting down roots in friendship and faith.

Seeing it all is suddenly to become aware of how fragmented English family life has become by comparison. It is rare to be asked to bless any homes other than those of immigrants. I can't help thinking that the Filipino people model in themselves a vision of community that seems so attractive and admirable amid the deprived appearance of the estate. So many of them work all the hours God sends; they find joy in raising families and still never miss Mass on Sunday, often coming straight from a long shift on the ward. They are a real inspiration.

I cannot stay long at the party as I have Confessions and the evening Mass to occupy me. As I am locking the church after these, the couple come by with a huge "doggy bag" of food from their feast and an offering for the church. How amazingly thoughtful of them.

The candidates for the local election have been canvassing. It is interesting to see their startled reaction to a clerical collar when I open the door. Even the man from the Christian People's Alliance looked somewhat taken-aback. I find the state of local politics even more depressing than national politics, perhaps because one is naive enough to imagine that at local level the concrete interests of real people might actually make a significant impact on the process. The twin obsessions locally seem to be with recycling and creating systems to cripple the flow of traffic. Meanwhile planning policy seems perverse and partial towards corporate interest; faith schools are under attack; and the care of the elderly barely seems to figure at all in any manifesto, with the exception of that of the Christian People's Alliance.

Some years ago the Government cleverly off-loaded the residential care of the elderly away from the NHS on to local authorities, thereby delaying the meltdown that is inevitable with such an ageing population. Thus the state can shift the tax burden further onto local authorities, which are also increasingly charging for services to the elderly in their own homes.

I am so fed-up with the endless verbiage about creating safer, cleaner communities, working to build a better borough etc. When will they learn that councils and political initiatives do not create communities? People do – people like my Filipino couple, living decent, hardworking, moral lives and literally making society by the way they embrace the gift of children and care for them. Local government does little to support them, beyond contributing towards the education of their children and collecting their rubbish.

Yet there they are, in the midst of that feral estate, embodying the kind of values that would transform it and having to pay nearly £1,500 council tax for their tiny little house out of nurses' salaries. What monstrous folly for the council to talk about creating community on the basis that what binds us together is our conviction that cars are evil and so too is throwing away tin cans and bottles.

I celebrated two years in my parish last week. It has gone incredibly quickly. There is much to thank God for here, and much still to be done. I think of the psalmist's conviction that unless the Lord builds the house, in vain do the builders labour. An awareness that this is so might be what emerges as the strain running through these muddled reflections on another week, another year.

School Trip

I spent Monday to Friday on the Isle of Wight, on School Journey with Year 6. That is, in education-speak, the last year of primary school.

The children have all finished their SATS and are suddenly looking almost too grown up for the school but it wasn't all sweetness and light. By the time we turned onto the motorway my hair was beginning to stand on end with the language and the content of the conversation.

I didn't realise I was so out of touch. I suppose I had not reckoned with the growing influence of television, in particular. Some of the children told me they watched more than six hours of television a day, including things I wouldn't. There was something more too, though, and it was only later that I realised there had to be another factor which explained the content of much of their conversation. A chance remark revealed that reproduction had recently been covered in science. Everything fell into place. This was why they could talk of nothing else. It was plain that many of them were simply not mature enough to make sense of the information they had been given as "science". Their obsession represented the need to tame something that had disturbed them deeply. I am not sure what this says about sex-education policy.

Each morning then I came downstairs to the unusual combination of a cooked breakfast in the dining room with 30 boisterous youngsters. Once the children were fed and in some cases medicated, we would board our coach. The Isle of Wight has a slightly unnerving feel to it, a bit like time travel. For all is familiar, it's just like the England you are used to, and yet it's not.

The "not" part I can't quite name: it's partly the architecture, the townscapes are not dominated by office blocks; there are hardly any tall buildings and the shop fronts are old fashioned, not all steel and neon. I didn't see any huge supermarkets, and there still seem to exist high streets and market squares without the ubiquitous high street brand names I am used to. The pace of life seemed slower, but perhaps we always project that feeling onto the places where we go on holiday.

Carisbrooke Castle, with its battlements and gift shop, was judged a generous "OK" by the children. Osborne House with its lack of interactivity and its requirement of some contextual knowledge left most of them cold. I personally found it very touching and realised what a very pious and sentimental lady Queen Victoria must have been; in every room were religious pictures and pictures of her children and grandchildren. We all seemed to like Alum Chine with its chairlift down to the shore.

We duly admired the seams of coloured sands in the cliff, for which the place is celebrated and from there took a boat trip out to the Needles. The combination of sea air, the rocking of the boat and probably little sleep, made them all look suddenly very drowsy. They all revived for the disco in the evening.

This seems to be turning into a, "I don't know what young people are coming to," diatribe. In truth it's as much about us and our society and to what extent Catholic education can and should be counter-cultural.

The girls spent hours putting on make-up and dressing themselves in the kinds of fashions that were clearly adult in conception and designed to emphasise their physicality. Several of their tops bore the FCUK trademark. The boys spent nearly as long preparing, though the results were less obvious. They then proceeded to follow the usual ritual of sitting on the opposite sides of the room whilst the DJ played such juvenile delights as "It's Raining Men, Hallelujah". In an age that claims to be serious about the protection of children, it seems incredible that we should regard television, fashion and pop-culture as harmless, but the adults, parents and teachers, looked on smiling indulgently. Am I alone in feeling uncomfortable about 11 year-olds dancing to "You're my Sex Bomb"?

Throughout the week there were marvellous moments, the kind of thing naively I expected of children on a school trip: running on the beach at night, a theme park visit, clandestine midnight feasts interrupted by irate teachers; stuff I expected. And then so much that I didn't expect. It feels like the Isle of

Wight, slightly unnerving. For the familiar landscape of childhood is evident still, and yet it's not. It is as if a kind of fog looms over it that changes the lineaments of childish faces and muffles childish sounds, and then suddenly, gloriously lifts again; a fog blown from a distant, more fallen world; the world of adults.

The denial of death's indignity

A couple of glorious sunny days bring a glimpse of summer, which then seems to fade as quickly as it came. The sunshine kindles my annual enthusiasm for gardening, which usually lasts a short time also. I like the idea of lots of things growing and flowering, but there's an awful lot of spadework involved. It's a bit like one's spiritual life. As it is, the rain comes all too soon and too heavy so that I walk to the hospital down a pavement carpeted with fallen blossoms of the most exquisite pinks and shades of white. It is a kind of bridal scene which seems rather to mock me as I hasten to a patient in the Intensive Care Unit (ITU).

I find visiting patients in ITU very difficult. It is not just because they are so ill and in many cases rendered unconscious. It is something about the feeling which you can get here, that you are in a sort of controlled sanctuary where the medics are the cultic elders and you are here on sufferance. There are rituals – the washing and wearing of plastic aprons – all of which, I am sure, are very necessary but which add to a sense of unreality, and when one comes to the bedside and finds someone swathed in tubes it is hard to see the person there in the midst of all the technology and the care.

I have negotiated an opt-out of wearing gloves when I am giving the Sacrament of the Sick. It would negate one of the most beautiful aspects of the sacrament – this healing touch which is *in persona Christi*. I know that the staff are thinking of the patient's good, but if I scrub up appropriately it seems to me that this good must be helped by the fact that they feel that contact of skin on skin, which psychologists tell us is one of the most basic of all human needs.

I am fortunate that at the hospital there are so many wonderful Catholic nurses. The sister on ITU is just a shining example of a wonderful Catholic professional and is so welcoming and supportive in this strange, high-powered, hi-tech environment.

I reflected on my reaction to the patients in ITU and thought about the seductive-sounding argument proposed in the Joffe Bill for "a death with dignity". It seemed to me, as I anointed the man on ITU this morning, that it was the medical procedures themselves which deprived him of dignity. Now, I am sure they were saving his life – that's the point: just because something is undignified it doesn't mean it is insupportable. It's hard to be dignified in the utilitarian sense in which the word is used in this context when you have tubes coming out of your nose, mouth, throat, chest and elsewhere, and when you are surrounded by machines that beep on a bed which looks more like a ride from a theme park.

When this is how we treat serious illness, I am curious to know why one would imagine that death should be devoid of the effects of serious physical or mental decay. It seems to me rather akin to suggesting that children should skip puberty as it involves all kinds of difficulties and behaviour not compatible with being a mature adult. The notion of death with dignity is almost a contradiction in terms, unless one sees death as a natural good. The process of supporting the dying in every way possible by good palliative and spiritual care is something quite different – it is the same thing which allows my man in ITU to put up with his indignity – they are treating his symptoms, and as long as they do so they are upholding his dignity.

Of course, in a society which has lost any sense of man as a transcendent reality dignity itself becomes utilitarian. Whenever we leave ideas about life being God-given out of the equation it is our anthropology that suffers and man who is reduced in value.

There is very little that is dignified about the death of soldiers in war in the narrow sense the word is used today. What dignifies it is clearly the sacrifice involved, the love for others, the bravery. It is something about the person, rather than the circumstances, that confers dignity. The same may be said for the martyr. It is significant that in both cases what actually conveys dignity is the fact that death is the unintended outcome of their suffering. Neither death itself nor even the manner of it is what conveys dignity; therefore, it must be to do with personal integrity, with life.

The challenge is always, as for me, to see the person amid the sickness and the paraphernalia of medical care. If for a moment I thought that part of that medical paraphernalia included the means for the patient to kill themselves, all that apparatus of care, which even seems to make it hard to see the person, would become something truly fearful, for its intended outcome could be something wholly different. It is no longer the patient's symptoms but their fate that is addressed by the medical profession.

The jealous critics of faith schools

I answered the phone to one of the frequent "How do I get my children baptised?" enquiries.

I normally ask preliminary questions, such as do you come to Mass here? Which parish do you live in? Hearing the plural "children", I was more directly inquisitive than I might otherwise have been and asked for their ages. They were three and four. Why haven't they yet been baptised?

"Well, I'll be honest," came the reply, "they have been baptised as Anglicans, but I wanted to get them baptised Catholic as they're on a waiting list for the Catholic school and I thought it would help their chances. It's what everyone else I know is doing, and you've got to play the system, haven't you?"

I thanked her for her frankness, and sympathised with her desire to get her children into a decent school. Her honesty had saved us both from committing sacrilege and deception. She was actually quite tearful and said she knew that it was the wrong thing to do, but she just wanted a good school for her children. It was her contention that her friends had gone down this route which shook me to the marrow.

I also wish the opponents of faith schools could realise the injustice of their views. The notion that, as faith groups, we get some kind of unfair advantage is a wholly false one. The reality is that faith schools create that advantage, the "value-added" element to education.

This is why there is so much pressure for places in them, because they consistently perform well and have a vision of the whole person, which produces people with some degree of respect for themselves, for others and for higher values.

My caller, God love her, wasn't interested in building up the kingdom of God or fanatical about promoting a Catholic state. She just wanted a decent school for her child.

Instead of attacking faith schools, the critics ought to be asking why it is that other schools do not command the same degree of parental support. It is my suspicion that opposition to faith schools may not be motivated by a desire for justice, but rather by a kind of jealousy. Otherwise our leaders would be learning lessons from religious schools, not trying to starve them of oxygen.

Talking of schools, I celebrate the leavers' Mass for the Upper VI and we say farewell to another year. There's something so poignant about these young people on the threshold of the big, bad world that makes me feel terribly paternal.

I recognise that this is a complicated feeling; I am both inspired by their goodness and fear to see disappointment. I put a huge amount of effort into the sermon for the leavers' Mass. The second reading is from Chapter 13 of St Paul's letter to the Corinthians. I tell them that they stand at a moment of history. History for the Catholic is, according to St Paul, about the three things that last: what I have believed, what I hope for, whom I love. It is not just about which exams I pass, which university I go to and what job I get.

Amid a huge variety of circumstances and possibilities, which seem at times random and arbitrary, there is an "I" created by God to believe, hope and love. The meaning of my history, then, is interpersonal.

"Each of us is the result of a thought of God. Each of us is willed, each of us is loved, each of us is necessary," says the Holy Father. You do not need to become Prime Minister or Pope to make an impact on the history of the world, I tell them. Already, merely by being who you are, a person of faith, hope and love, you make history. This is what we celebrate today, what I offer on the paten in the Mass. And history is charged with the polarity of redemption: what I believe, what I hope, is that love will make me less closed in on myself and more open to the life and truth which comes from beyond, from the one in whose image we are made.

On Saturday we celebrate First Holy Communion in the parish. This is invariably preceded by a call to the hospital in the small hours and I am left virtually on automatic pilot, for the day, which is a shame. Perhaps it is this exhaustion that gives me the foolish idea that one can see the workings of grace. Why is it that some children just seem to be more aware, more recollected, more in awe, more pious than others? Is it nature or super-nature? Is it about degrees of intelligence or maturity?

Obviously, family practice has something to do with it, but it is impossible not to be struck by the evident piety in some and the lack of it in others. After the flowers and the partying, I wonder how many of these children will be at Mass next week and regularly thereafter.

I am scandalised by that in the real sense – not meaning I am censorious of those who do not come – I just can't get over it. I can see that it might be difficult for some families. What I cannot understand is how, having ensured your child has received Holy Communion once, it thereafter becomes a matter of indifference.

June

All My Hope

As I enter the church there is the sound of African music and the sight of wonderful African women in amazingly coloured dresses, their huge headdresses swaying gently to the music. In the sacristy fifty priests are vesting, from the crisply amiced to the nylon-zipped according to age and predilection. Some kind of uniformity has been imposed by the arrival of concelebration chasubles borrowed from Westminster Cathedral. There are some familiar faces here from seminary days, many of whom one never sees except at ordinations and funerals.

We process into the church and the roof is being raised with All My Hope on God is Founded, surely a good sentiment with which to begin an ordination ceremony. There is the candidate vested in his deacon's stole, standing in the front bench next to his parents till the moment when he is solemnly invited to come and stand before the bishop.

I imagine that married couples must feel the same at weddings, but seeing him stand there, hands joined, it is impossible not to be taken back to my own ordination day. Seeing it happen to someone else makes it all the more real for you. So overwhelming was the moment that one's appreciation was inadequate, it needs to deepen and be assimilated day by day, year by year.

I listen as the candidate answers the bishop's questions. They provide me with a timely vade-mecum with which to review my own life: "Are you resolved to celebrate the mysteries of Christ faithfully and religiously as the Church has handed them down to us for the glory of God and the sanctification of Christ's people?"

I think of the awe one had approaching the altar for one's first Mass and how the rust of habit corrodes that. I reflect too, on how difficult I find it to say three Masses in a day and still be appropriately focused. I think of the raucous family Masses where one can hardly hear oneself and ask myself have I celebrated these "religiously"?

"Are you resolved to exercise the ministry of the word worthily and wisely, preaching the Gospel and explaining the

Catholic Faith?" asks the bishop.

One of the things I have found hardest about being a priest is that I get very few opportunities, beyond the Sunday sermon, to explain the Catholic faith. I explained it far more in the days when I was a school teacher. It has been my experience in parish life that most catechesis is done by lay people, and is jealously guarded. Even in the formation of adult converts my input is "a resource" to be called on when required. Sometimes after my allotted ten minutes a catechist will "sum up" and "with all due respect" will contradict what I have said, quoting the canon of their own experience.

"Are you resolved to consecrate your life to God for the salvation of his people and to unite yourself more closely every day to Christ the High Priest, who offered himself for us to the Father as a perfect sacrifice?"

I am, with the help of God, replies the candidate. And what more can any of us say? Well, one can resolve to put one's back into it again, with the same fervour and idealism with which the man standing there does it today. I have found the Devil tempts one to take back the gift in a thousand ways: becoming "too tired" to pray, seeking recreation outside the Creator, being impatient with the demands of the phone or doorbell, craving affirmation and success; forgetting that the meaning of one's true life is hidden with Christ in God.

And then the candidate prostrates himself on the sanctuary floor and we call on the Church of heaven in the litany of the saints. For me it is the most profound gesture of service and dedication I can think of, to lie on the earth from which God made you, so you may be taken over by the Spirit of God to become in your own body a pontifex, a bridge between God and man. You are not alone in this; heaven already reaches out to you, the saints pray for you and urge you to think of the life lived on the heights. You must believe that all things are possible to God, for however much you analyse your own choice or sell it short, most truly He chose you, and you must prostrate yourself humbly before this choice. No matter that in what follows sometimes you may feel very close to the earth. Reflect that it is from there you started and it was only He who raised you up, who fills the starving with good things and raises the lowly.

Celebrating Mass in the dark Tower

The Tower of London has a rather jolly atmosphere these days. As Britain's most popular attraction for foreign tourists it is thronged with sightseers, people relaxed and on holiday. The Yeoman Warders in their Elizabethan costume seem to blend easily with the actors dressed up to provide atmosphere. On Friday it was basking in blistering heat and there was a band playing beside the river. I was there with a group of Year 10s (fourth year secondary school children). We had come less for the tourist experience and more for one of the Tower's most precious associations for Catholics. For we had been granted the privilege of visiting and holding Mass in the cell where St Thomas More was imprisoned for 15 months before his execution.

The Yeoman Gaoler met us and gave a brilliant introduction to the Tower and its history. He had that instinct which makes young people attend – he treated them as though they were more adult and more intelligent than they were, asking them some quite obscure questions about history and then, when they didn't know an answer, saying in a tone that suggested mock despair: "You really should get out more, lads" – all delivered in a mild Scots accent. A long row of medal ribbons on his chest hinted that his present quaint uniform was something he had come to after long service in others.

Thomas More and John Fisher were both kept in the Bell Tower, which is the first thing you come to through the present tourist entrance at the West Gate. The Gaoler reminded us that in the 16th century just yards from More's cell would have been the noise and bustle of coin manufacture, for the Royal Mint was within the precincts of the Tower. Other things I had heard once and forgotten were that Rudolf Hess was imprisoned there during the Second World War and that they were continuing to execute spies there up until that time. Such details are meat and drink to the boys, of course.

The gaoler showed us into More's cell. It was larger that I had expected – about 18 ft long in all, pentagonal in shape with a rough stone floor, vaulted roof and recessed bays which ended in arrow-slit windows cut in the walls which were up to 15 ft thick in places. Through these narrow slits More glimpsed the comings and goings at the gate. He recounted in a letter how he had seen the brothers from the London Charterhouse being led out to their execution. They held hands and sang, "like bridegrooms going to a wedding". They must have both encouraged him and made him fearful of his own constancy. Shafts of light came through these narrow windows – it was a very bright and sunny day – but electric lights meant it was hard to tell just how dark it must have been for More. Outside it was, in fact, the hottest May day for decades. Inside it was very cool which was a comfort to us but an intimation of how cold it must have been in winter. In fact to visit such a place is really to have little idea of what it must actually be like to be incarcerated for months on end, especially in the knowledge that you held your destiny in your hands and that with some mental equivocation or reservation you might sign the Act of Supremacy as so many friends and colleagues, so many bishops, priests and lay people already had.

On the deep sill of one of the bays I set up the things for Mass and vested. It was through this action that we were truly to enter into solidarity with St Thomas More. We prepared for Mass by saying a decade of the rosary and with some readings from Peter Ackroyd's wonderful biography. He speaks of More prostrating himself in his cell, meditating on Christ in Gethsemane and hoping that "I will hear what Our Lord will speak within me." Ackroyd goes on to lament the damage caused by the Reformation: "Perhaps the Lord spoke to him of a time, soon to come, when there would be no more lights and images, no more pilgrimages, and processions, no guild plays and no more ringing for the dead, no maypoles or Masses or holy water, no birch at midsummer and no roses at Corpus Christi." He sounds a salutary reminder of how deep such customs touch the human psyche and how much we lose when we lose such popular piety.

Then we celebrated Mass, the boys extraordinarily recollected and prayerful, kneeling on that same rough stone floor. As I held up the host at the elevation I glimpsed through the narrow arrow slit the vista beyond the curtain wall up to Tower Hill. I saw the offices of the merchant bank where I once worked, and where one day I recognised that God was calling me to priesthood.

It was one of those rare moments of seeing how God's Providence has held you by the hand; a moment of great peace. I am sure the example and the intercession of St Thomas More helped many there to find that narrow window to the Divine that makes us long for a freedom like his.

A short break from the parish

It was an average sort of week really, spent celebrating the sacraments, visiting the sick, paying the bills, dealing with marriage papers, listening to stories of imaginary demonic possession and dealing with family feuds over funeral arrangements. All that was out of the ordinary was the chance to get away for a couple of days, as it was half-term and I had no school on Friday.

The moment I went "off-call" on Wednesday evening I was in the car, heading for the hills, or at least for a place called Crudwell in Wiltshire, and a B&B in a former rectory.

It was still light by the time I arrived, and in the grand surroundings of the rectory with its walled garden and church clock chiming nearby I felt a breath of summer peace.

After a hearty breakfast the next morning, I drove into Malmesbury to visit what remains of Malmesbury Abbey. The abbey was of Saxon foundation; St Aldhelm was its first abbot and it had already been a religious house for seven centuries or more when it was surrendered to the Crown at the Dissolution some 470 years ago.

I was irritated to see that the information sheet glossed this event as the church "was given back to the town" to be its parish church. Very little of the Norman church remains; much of what is now the parish church is a Victorian rebuild, but one can get a feeling of what a magnificent building it must have been from the beautiful carved portal of the porch and its representation of what I assume is a scene from the Apocalypse, with an angel soaring above the elders sounding a trumpet.

Some of the outer walls survive with their blind arcading, and a wall of what was once the huge transept now stands looking for all the world like a piece of gargantuan stage scenery. Its handsome windows are open to the weather and weeds grow from niches in its "bare ruined choirs".

I am a bit of an aficionado of English country towns with their tea shops, antique shops and Miss Marple ambience, and I will never neglect to pay a visit to the ancient parish church. In Malmesbury – very much a picture postcard sort of town with its market cross and stone houses – one is suddenly aware of an England in which Catholic religious life was woven into the fabric of the land. Here, for example, the centre of the town was not the sober, understated piety of the parish church but the beating heart of a religious house with the shrine of a saint and a regimen of prayer day and night; the echoes dying not those of the English Hymnal and the Book of Common Prayer, but the ancient Gregorian chant and the sacred mutter of the Mass. I know many will dismiss this as mere nostalgia but it is impossible not to feel some vague sense of alienation on entering such a place, of being disconcerted by what, by rights, should be familiar but which disconcerts you by its likeness to something you can't quite remember. It is like finding again the house where you were born and discovering it has been made into a museum, all very correct and nicely done, but somehow obscuring what it was originally intended for.

In what were the abbey grounds, leading down to the river, is the most beautiful garden; billed as the most extensive rose-garden in Europe. I think I was about a week or so early for the roses, but it was a delightful place, and there was something profoundly relaxing about wandering in the gardens. I reflected that in biblical terms gardening does not constitute work in the way that agriculture does. It made my fingers itch to do more in my little patch of garden, and to begin by renewing all-out warfare on the squirrels who now seem to be eating my herbs and jumping up and down on my seedlings.

I then headed on to Lacock. This is a village entirely in the care of the National Trust and therefore something like a time-capsule with its ancient cottages and streets unmarked with yellow lines or traffic signs. No wonder that they use it so much for filming period dramas like Pride and Prejudice. Here too there was once an abbey which was sold to become a private house. This is sadder than ever, somehow. Its splendid eighteenth century salons are built around the fan-vaulted monastic cloister.

It was the ancestral home of the photographic pioneer Henry Fox Talbot.

I came back to the parish in time for Exposition and evening Mass for the Feast of the Sacred Heart. We had a most beautiful Mass with my youth choir singing Jesu Dulcis Memoria, and those wonderful, if slightly sentimental hymns: "To Jesus Heart All Burning" and "O Sacred Heart".

The altar was covered in roses and peonies and lilies. It seemed the perfect feast for a summer's evening. It is a feast in which the sun of God's love for us is closest and full and warming, its days are longest and there is rest and peace.

Flowers for Remembrance

You never know quite what to expect when you open the front door. In a sense we take a lot for granted. I read a statistic recently that suggested that you are more likely to be assaulted as a clergyman than you are as a policeman. I don't know if it's true. Thank God I have never been assaulted though I have been threatened. It isn't all like that. I have also opened the door and been presented with jars of homemade marmalade or chocolate fudge cakes from kind parishioners worrying that I am wasting away.

I opened the door to one poor man who told me he only had 45 minutes to live. For the next half hour he spun a tale of woe, which, like most of them, ended with a demand for £40 so he could buy some good strong shoes so he could resume his work as a security guard. Another man wanted to speak to a priest about his spiritual torment and then wanted to show me the scars from his many operations. On balance, he too, decided that his needs were more temporal than spiritual and on that occasion I was taken in by circumstantial evidence of his bona fides and his sworn assurances of swift repayment and "lent" him some money. The sad thing about such encounters is I realise that each time they happen I become that bit more cynical about people's hard luck stories. I stand there waiting for the magic words, "Could you help me out, Father?"

Tuesday's encounter was more positive. I opened the door to an elderly Italian lady who was in some distress. I brought her in and sat her down and little by little she told me she had just come from her GP. He was telling her that she was showing signs of the onset of Alzheimer's disease. Clearly she was very upset about this and her distress was channelling itself in a particular direction. Her doctor, she said, had completely dismissed something she was sure was true.

She told me that she had shared with him a very strong memory of early childhood. Her mother was abroad and she had been sent to board at a convent school in Desio, near Milan.

There was great excitement one day because a cardinal was coming to visit the school. He was visiting Desio because he had been born there and his mother still lived there. This lady, now 88, was selected to present a bouquet to the cardinal. Overawed by the whole experience and given to outbursts of temper, she had thrown it at his feet. The nuns never forgave her, she said, not only because he was a cardinal, but because he later became the Pope. She was sure this was an accurate memory; her doctor told her she was fantasising. It was vital for her to source this memory; she asked me if there was any way I could help her. It was time for me to go and say Mass so I took her phone number and promised to call later.

I did a bit of checking on the internet, and discovered that Achille Ratti, born in Desio, was Cardinal Archbishop of Milan when my lady would have been no more than five or six years old. In 1922 when she was seven, he became Pope Pius XI. It looked as if her memory was an accurate one. I phoned her with the good news that it seemed highly probable that history confirmed her memory.

I asked her what the cardinal was like and how he reacted to the projectile posie of flowers. "He was nice," she said. "He smiled and said, 'Benedica ti fanciulla', and blessed me." But the poor nuns were mortified and never forgave her, apparently. She went on to talk about how profoundly unhappy she had been there. She didn't see her mother for five years. I couldn't help wondering how much of a factor such unhappiness might be in people whose memories begin to fail them. Perhaps it is the mind's way of protecting itself.

It clearly helped her to know that she had not simply imagined the circumstances she had described. I found it a very touching story. But I also know that it is symptomatic of Alzheimer's that patients can remember their childhood when they can't remember what happened yesterday, so I am not sure what it means for her prognosis. Perhaps this is what the doctor was trying to tell her.

Seeing this lady anxious, confused and frail as she told her story I had suddenly a very clear picture of the scene she had described; of the awkward, unhappy child and the smiling prelate whose blessing stayed in her mind. Perhaps he will bless her now from heaven, where memory can no longer hurt, since nothing that is good or lovely will ever be lost again.

July

Facing death like the saints

It was Sunday evening and, as it happened, I was in the hospital anyway, taking Holy Communion to someone, when my bleeper went off. I am learning to live with the bleeper and have become conditioned, in Pavlovian fashion, to jump to attention when it goes off. I am beginning to notice how many bleeps there are in the twenty-first century day. Mobile phones, reversing vehicles, computers, train doors and microwave ovens all bleep, causing me to start wildly.

I was being summoned to the Accident and Emergency Department. An elderly man had collapsed at a bus stop with a massive stroke. They knew only his name. Then the doctor showed me something on a chain round the man's neck. It was a medallion with a picture of Our Lady on it and on the other side the words, "I am a Catholic. In the event of accident or illness please call a priest." To the great credit of the A&E staff they had done so immediately as their solemn duty, and his Guardian Angel saw to it that I was three minutes down the corridor.

In my mind I was 10 years old again, transported back to a rather dingy classroom in the De la Salle brothers' school. Our form teacher, a layman called Mr Jones, was giving us a religious instruction lesson in which he expounded the Catechism to us. After looking at the questions on extreme unction he was urging us to always carry a rosary or something which identified us as Catholics in case we were ever involved in an accident or taken ill. What impressed itself on my mind then was the sense of priority. My childhood mind, capable of any number of fantasies of disaster worthy of International Rescue or Captain Scarlet now saw the real drama, not in terms of the danger to life and limb, but the danger to the immortal soul of dying uncomforted by the grace of the sacraments. The fact that I remember the advice so vividly suggests that it made a big impression on me at the time. As with all these things, however, one always imagines that they only happen to other people. None of us really plans on a sudden, unprovided death; we imagine we will have time to prepare.

Seeing this man, I remembered Mr Jones and that advice of long ago. I found the holy oil and the ritual to give the last rites to this man about whom I knew nothing except his name and his kinship in the mystical Body of Christ.

I always think of Mr Jones on the Feast of St Maria Goretti. Again it was a religious instruction class and one hot summer afternoon – probably her feast day on July 6 – he read the story of her life to us. The story was only half-finished when the bell sounded for the end of school. Instead of the usual stirring caused by the bell there was a silence and stillness of intense interest and concentration. He said we could either stay and finish the story now or we could finish it at the next lesson. To a boy, we asked him to finish the story before we went home that day. Again, it made a deep impression on me. She was a child after all, and a saint. Her murderer and her mother had both been at her canonisation. Mr Jones had been there too, when he was but a young teacher. Maria was not some figure from a remote past. As with accidents, so also with sanctity, one is inclined to think such things only happen to other people. Suddenly hearing about a child barely older than myself, the story set me to thinking about sanctity as something that could happen in real life and not just the remote, two-dimensional world of history.

Indeed, celebrating the feast of Maria Goretti this year I reflected that she seems more contemporary than ever. The Church of the 1950s focussed on her heroic virtue in defending her purity against violent assault. The Church of today is coming to terms with the extent of insidious, secretive assaults on the purity of young people, even within her ranks. St Maria Goretti must surely be the special patron for all children who are victims of abuse, whose martyrdom is of a different kind: of the slow, daily, unremitting kind of living with the pain of the past and learning to trust again, to allow themselves to be loved.

I visited St Maria Goretti's shrine at Nettuno a few years ago. The countryside round about is still poor – you would hardly imagine you are in a rich industrialised nation; the roads are tracks in many places, the houses have tin roofs, the land is brown and dry and scrubby yielding little. And there in a basilica by the blue Mediterranean lies the little saint who long ago woke in me a sense that there is something glorious about holiness, stronger than death, outshining life.

Saints trust that in the event of accident or danger there is one who is always with them to rescue them, to keep them safe, whatever threatens. This hope is like a seal on their heart, or perhaps, a medallion round their neck; the hope that makes it possible to embrace life.

Witnessing to the Gospel of Life

There are many Filipino families in the parish and there will be a baptism every week until August of one of their number. It is their work in the hospital which has brought the Filipinos here and from my point of view it makes for a wonderful atmosphere there. I imagine it was similar in the Fifties when there were many Irish nurses at work. It is so nice to go onto a ward and to be greeted with a warm smile and a "Hello, Father". I was called to a dying man the other night and the nurse who had called me came and knelt by his bed and prayed with me as I said the commendation for the dying. What care she showed for her patient – what the health service jargon now terms "holistic care".

Like so many other things now included in mission statements, it has been going on as long as there have been good people working in the health service. Indeed, the Sisters of Mercy who went to nurse with Florence Nightingale in the Crimea were practising "holistic care" 140 years ago, long before it had been thought of as a performance target. But I digress.

Sunday's baby was baptised Rose-Marie. I had visited the family in their home earlier in the week. Though spotlessly clean it was shabby and very sparsely furnished. At seven o'clock the husband was just arriving home from his work in a factory some 20 miles away. He travels there by bus. The wife works in the intensive care unit in the hospital.

They were cheerful and pleasant and effusively grateful for my visit. "We never expected the priest to come to us," they said. So we duly celebrated the baptism with friends present and the usual Filipino custom of having at least a dozen godparents. Afterwards the couple gave me an extremely generous donation.

They had invited all their friends to a local Chinese restaurant for a meal and they invited me too. Their hospitality enabled me to get to know more people. The Filipinos aren't exactly shy; but they are, I would say, deferential. They greet me after Mass but don't often linger to chat, so it was lovely to have the opportunity to spend some time with them. I felt it was important as they make up a significant number of my flock. Moreover, they are exiles and they need the support of the Church. Their hearts must need be divided. "All of us are supporting two families," one man said to me. "One here and one back at home." How they do this on nursing salaries I do not know, and while they are clearly a huge asset to the hospital, something in me is uneasy that we should continue to staff a health service by employing people whose standard of living at home is so low that it renders a poor English salary acceptable to them.

Some of them have to leave spouses and even children behind in the Philippines until they have managed to establish themselves here. Some live in nurses' accommodation provided by the hospital, others have moved out; many couples share a flat.

There was something deeply edifying about spending time with these joyful, gentle people whose vocation is caring, and who have left home and loved ones far away so that they may better support them. It strikes me that they are living very unselfish lives; that they are far removed from our own culture of looking after number one.

Gently they spoke about how surprised they are by the number of elderly people who live alone here, and how odd it is that so many people have to live in old people's homes. The care of the elderly was clearly something they regard as the prerogative of the family, not the state. To them, family life means much more than the nuclear family – families are extended. I asked one woman what she missed most and she said: "My cousins. Back at home there was always someone to be with, someone to talk to, or to help you."

On the day declared "A Day for Life" by the Bishops' Conference, I felt I had been shown something very profound. As ever, the Holy Father is surely prophetic in his assertion that surrounding the actual issues of euthanasia, abortion or contraception, there is a culture. These issues are the barometers of the value we place on children or the elderly from day to day. If the life of old people is a burden and a trouble to your own pleasure and ability to get on, then of course you will soon look for selfish solutions. Our culture has developed a "What's in it for me?" approach. This is deathly, for that which I seek within myself is bound to die.

I asked them to tell me what the parish could do to support the Filipino community. "Would you like to have a Filipino Mass once in a while?" I wondered.

"Oh yes," they cried, "then we could sing our Filipino songs."

I will talk to the national Filipino chaplain and see if it can be arranged. I would love them to be able to sing their songs, but in their witness to the Gospel of Life it seems to me they are already singing the songs of Zion in an alien land.

A call that left me sick at heart

The timing made it even more shocking somehow. It was an exceptionally busy Sunday: three Masses, three baptisms, the hospital calls and a World Youth Day meeting in the evening. Looming somewhere in the back of my mind is the thought of going on holiday.

I was in the middle of my second baptism. It was a dear Filipino couple and their first baby, a two month old baby with almond eyes and jet black hair which stuck up on his crown like a comb. Filipino baptisms are always joyful occasions; very much family and community celebrations and one can take it as read that all there practise the faith. The baptism was particularly special because it is probably the last time I will see this couple. They, along with several of their compatriots are moving to a part of the country where they stand some chance of getting a mortgage on nursing salaries. I totally understand why they must do it, but I am so sorry to see them go.

It is awful when the hospital bleeper goes in the middle of Mass or, in this case, a baptism. With the best will in the world it is hard not to have your concentration and prayerfulness totally shattered by it. You immediately are conscious that you need to get to the end so that you can find out if it is a dire emergency.

So it was that I finished the baptism and said to the couple, who being nurses know the score, that I would just find out who was bleeping me and come back to have a photograph taken. Back in the house I called the switchboard and was put through to the delivery suite on maternity. One of the midwives told me that a Catholic woman was having a "termination" that afternoon and wanted me to come and bless the baby afterwards. I was just stunned. I could barely get my head round such a statement. I tried to be calm and professional and said that I was sorry, but there was no way I could come and bless the child in those circumstances. I would happily come and speak to the mother, pray with her, even. I was told crisply that there was no question of being able to change her mind, the "process", as she termed it, had already begun. Still rather numb from this I returned to church to stand and pose with the couple and their newly baptised child.

The midwives called me twice more that afternoon, after the operation was completed. I explained calmly and carefully that I did not feel able to come. "This isn't a decision she has come to lightly," I was told by them. "Could you explain what difference that has made to the child?" I asked. I was told I was putting them in an impossible situation. "This woman is a Roman Catholic and has requested a blessing for her child." I could see it was an impossible situation, for in the modern, totally subjective response to the issue, it was the mother's take on reality which alone was to be maintained and respected at all costs. She was their patient.

I have been examining my reactions and my conscience ever since. Should I have gone? But the going was not the issue; I offered on each occasion to speak to the parents, but it was a blessing for the newly aborted baby that was required. Such a blessing could be of no spiritual benefit to a dead child who, as I explained to the midwives already, had every claim on God's mercy. A blessing would be for the benefit of the mother, and, I felt, would be in some way to collude in what she had done. The request for a blessing seemed a clear indication the mother realised this was a child. It would be entirely for the benefit of the mother, to have the effect of, in some way, making her feel better about what she had done, in practice blessing it. I felt I could not do it.

I cannot judge the mother's state of mind or soul, but it was these and her needs which were the basis of an appeal to my compassion – both that of the midwives and the workings of my own conscience. Against that I am certain that to take the life of an unborn child is an intrinsic moral evil. Paradoxically the mother's anxiety to have the child blessed might argue for some knowledge of this.

How do I interface with a health system which recognises no such thing as this intrinsic evil? A system which next week will ask me to sign a certificate of blessing and commemoration for a woman who has miscarried at 12 weeks to comfort her for the baby she has lost, but is this afternoon abetting a poor mother to kill her baby because her attitude towards it can deprive it, at a stroke, of its right to live? How can it be that in our so-called health service the same outcome is for one mother a tragedy to be succoured and for another a medical procedure to be facilitated? The same ethical roulette would not be tolerated when it came to say amputations, and yet day by day it happens in the hospital where I work and every similar hospital in the country.

I am sick at heart and I continue to ask myself was there something else I could have done. I can only pray for that mother and her child and commend them to the infinite mercy of God.

The Good Fight

Poor Peggy Mulligan is dead. She went into hospital a fortnight ago with an ulcerated leg and picked up a chest infection. She died peacefully, so her nephew told me on the phone. They were close; she had no children of her own, for she was a spinster – not the unhappy, thin-blooded caricature one associates with the word, but someone full of life and love, from a different age in which we still believed it possible to have no partner and yet be deeply fulfilled and happy.

Between her work as a nurse and her strong faith Peggy was a person rich in love. With St Paul she can say "I have fought the good fight, I have run the race to the finish, I have kept the faith."

I used to take Holy Communion to her each week; always ringing her to let her know when I would be arriving for it could take her several minutes to reach the front door of her neat little flat. I would give her Communion and then she would love to chat. She had one of those beautiful soft Irish brogues that I could have listened to for hours, indeed some days I believe she could have talked for hours but I had to tear myself away. It always amazes me, the difference between people whose take on life seems to be that the glass is half full and those for whom the glass is half empty. Loneliness and the deteriorations of old age seemed to Peggy to be reminders of how blessed she had been. To another they would be motives for complaint or excuses for self-pity, or they would have given rise to the incessant craving of sympathy.

Little by little, week by week, in bursts of a few minutes, one begins to build a relationship with people like Peggy who receive Holy Communion at home, until the visit becomes a fixed point in your week, as it clearly is in theirs. There will be a huge gap as I go on my rounds this week. What people forget is that the housebound receive you in a totally different way from those of us who are out and about being "useful" as we see it. Our business, our preoccupation and our activity mean that there is less space in us for others. They are contemplatives these old ladies; living their days in solitude filled with the nearness of God, and receptive to the presence of others.

So there are two funerals this week. It is always the way; not one funeral since Easter and now two in the same week. The first is of a man who died suddenly of an undetected ulcer. At the request of his family his is one of those sad half-services in the cemetery chapel. It's an odd chapel, with benches facing one another, it reminds me of the chapel of a Victorian public school with its red brick and heavy timbers and collegiate seating.

Out into the sunshine and the yews are the colour of wet velvet and the cemetery like a well-kept park. These are war graves we are passing; a rose bush between each neat headstone. I thought of the Charles Causley poem about the war cemetery in Bayeux. He speaks of the strange "geometry" of death. It is a pleasant sight, the neat little garden, as if the horror of these individual tragedies can somehow be softened by the years and the apparent return of order and neatness.

I am grateful that for once we process in silence. Too often the undertaker wants to chat. Apart from actually feeling it is important to pray as we go – there are some beautiful psalms for the procession to the graveside – I feel it must look very disrespectful to the family following behind in the cars to see minister and priest passing the time of day. It is as if we are players merely in some tragedy not really our own. Our strange clothes are part of a role required, but we can step out of role when not actually within earshot of the mourners. We lend our solemnity like minstrels. I hope to goodness it never becomes like that, just another funeral to be solemnly played.

I am shocked, as I give a blessing at the graveside, to see the undertaker cross himself. Afterwards I discover he is Polish. You know you are getting old when the undertakers look young, but he really does. He has only been in England a few months and yes, he is a Catholic. It makes a difference. I remember the one and only time the undertaker received Communion at a funeral. It really did make the whole thing feel different; no longer was he just part of some respectable protocol of death but a fellow believer. I felt this was no longer just "undertaking", somehow he had crossed a line and become involved.

August

On call

I was woken by my bleeper going off at 2.30am. For a brief, somnambulant moment I wonder why the alarm is going off when it is not yet light and then feel an adrenaline rush as I realise what it is and I am wide awake.

I call the hospital switchboard. A gentle, calm, night-time voice answers and apologises for disturbing me, which strikes me as rather thoughtful, considering it is my job. "Putting you through to Sussex Ward now," says the voice. "Mrs So-and-so is poorly and won't last until morning," comes the message. The name is a common one and unfamiliar to me. I get dressed clumsily and collect my pocket ritual, stole and sick call set, a gift from the Sisters of Mercy who looked after us in the seminary.

All of this seems to take a long time. Night stretches out the minutes. I drive the short distance to the hospital, my mind racing and arrive less than 15 minutes after I was called.

It is a strange world, the world of night. The hospital has lost all of its bustle and activity and is resting. There is a nocturnal population of staff going quietly about their business of watching over the sick and sleeping and I reflect that this world is one of which, by and large, we are heedless.

Do I ever think, as my day is ending and I settle down at night, of the nurses, the switchboard operatives, the ancillary staff all keeping vigil? Or even of those for whom the night will be their last, who will close their eyes for the last time on this world?

I think suddenly of all those who watch or wait tonight and I pray for them as one co-opted to their world.

Down the long and eerily silent corridors I hurry. The place is deserted, and yet when I reach the wards there is a curious sense of peace.

I realise it is because of the silence in a place I normally see full of activity. There seems to be a special kind of camaraderie among the staff too, who are sitting at the nurses' station, an oasis of light between the darkened bays of sleeping patients.

In a room by the nursing station is Madeleine, propped up and looking small amid a mound of pillows. She is breathing with great difficulty through an oxygen mask. She is unconscious, and as I look down I suddenly realise that I know who she is. I have seen her before.

I was on supply in her parish for several weeks when first ordained and I took Holy Communion to her each week, to her little cottage by the common, from where she would look out from her downstairs bedsit on the changing seasons. It seems to my mind a rather beautiful providence that it should not be some anonymous stranger to whom I have come in the night this first time, but someone with whom I have travelled briefly before.

I am alone with her in the little room with the nurses murmuring outside and beyond the window a city of a million lights flickering in the night. Perhaps it is the same for Madeleine – she alone, and beyond her in the darkness glimmer the million lights of heaven and somewhere in the background a murmuring: "Go forth Christian soul. May your home be this day in Zion." The ritual done, I sit with her and try to say the rosary but my mind wanders.

From time to time a nurse comes to check her. I feel a great sense of peace in the room. I stay till her carer arrives and then make my way back down the long corridors into the cool night air as the first glimmer of light shows in the east.

At home I make myself a milky drink and go back to bed, but I cannot get back to sleep. I feel full of all kinds of feelings; there is a sorrow and with it almost elation. Madeleine was full of years and deeply faithful. Every night the same drama is played out in the hospital, but this dying has been soothed, as her living was, by the ministry of the Church. And this is my involvement in it. I can minister the medicine which eases all pain, though in common humanity the thought of the pain frightens me.

It is light by the time I eventually doze off, but I can still probably get an hour and a half before I must be up and getting on with the day. When I wake, it is to the familiar routine of a Monday morning. I call the hospital and find that Madeleine died peacefully at 6am. I will pray for her at Mass, where dying Jesus destroyed our death, where darkness implodes on itself to become only light.

A Gentle Dying

Like an animal that knows it must soon hibernate, some pheromone, some chemical receptor in my brain tells me it is about time to have a holiday. Going away seems to get harder when I think of all the things I have to prepare. It is always easier to do things yourself, to follow your own routine than to hand that routine over to someone else. I will have to write endless notes for the supply priest, and then I am bound to forget something vital. The prospect of writing the bidding prayers for the next four weeks fills me with gloom, since there are only so many intentions you can come up with in one day. I loathe packing, and the difficulties of packing for holidays get more depressing than ever when you are worrying about taking a portable sacristy along with you too so that you can say Mass and assist at weddings whilst on holiday.

For all this, there is something deeper which resists going away, letting go. It is easy to become the victim of responsibility and always to find another reason why you cannot walk away. No sooner have I booked a flight than I hear that poor Mrs Lacey is fading fast. Some ridiculously selfish, childish part of me is resentful that she might die whilst I am away when I have never missed a week taking her Holy Communion. Now I am in a quandary as to whether to delay leaving for a couple of days until after her funeral.

Six months ago she would struggle to the door to let me in. Nowadays I let myself in with a key. I saw her on Thursday as usual and I thought she was very weak and breathless but put it down in part to the heat. Then her daughter called whilst I was in the confessional on Saturday night. I knew Mrs Lacey had a daughter but had the impression that she lived far away and didn't visit, but who can really know what goes on in families? Now the daughter asks if I will come and give her mother "Extreme Unction".

There follows a long unnecessary and, I feel, almost guilty speech about how she herself is not a believer in "established religions", but feels it might calm her mother; people of her mother's generation would find it a comfort, she was sure. I know only too well that her mother would want it with every ounce of strength left in her. I have seen the way her pained face relaxes and looks almost young when she receives the host week by week. Yes I agree; it is what her mother would want.

I go after the evening Mass, and am again greeted by the daughter with a worried formula about how she is a "spiritual person" but not necessarily a religious one. I suppose what she is expressing sounds like fear. The fact that we keep coming back to her own faith or lack of it, suggests that this is really the issue. The sacrament will give her mother "calm" in her own terms and that's acceptable. Maybe she is afraid that this calm might be a motive for credibility. Her words tell me she is determined to keep this faith of her mother's at a safe distance; what I think I may be hearing is something else; a regret that she does not still have it.

Mrs Lacey is drifting in and out of sleep, but when I tell her I have come to give her the Sacrament of the Sick she tries to sit up. I tell her to relax. She is such an independent spirit. Each week she would apologise profusely for not seeing me out; this poor lady who needed oxygen to walk to the kitchen. I realise suddenly that I do not even know her first name; it seemed fitting always to call her "Mrs Lacey".

Her breathing is painfully laboured. The intense heat must be so uncomfortable for her. She cannot swallow so her daughter gives her a swab with water on it from time to time. I invite the daughter to come and hold her mother's hand whilst I go through the ritual of anointing and then the commendation of the dying. Into the loneliness of the drama of this dying comes a calm, as the Church calls the Archangels and the Patriarchs and the martyrs and the saints to stand over her in the shabby room and ease her passing. There is something so grounded about the ritual; the use of touch, and the healing balm of holy oil. What matter if to the unbeliever I am apparently a conjurer performing a comforting illusion? I know deep in my being that this touches what is most real and it is the failing body which is the illusion. No sooner have

I finished than the old lady relaxes into a deep sleep and her breathing eases.

Mrs Lacey's daughter called me early on Sunday morning to say that her mother had died peacefully during the night. With a catch in her voice she told me, "She died clutching her rosary." I will bury her on Friday, God rest her.

Fixing my gaze on the wholeness of God

On the feast of St John Vianney, patron saint of parish clergy, I am far from my parish and the cure of souls, on holiday in Somerset. I am putting a bit of time in on my own soul, drinking in the peace of the countryside in great, grateful draughts. I celebrate Mass in the house where I am staying with a view through an old leaded window out across Exmoor down to the coast.

The immemorial hills are softened by the summer light so that the variegated greens of tree and meadow and the dun and purple moor are like the fold of some vast quilt across a sleeping giant. The hills seem as living, breathing things. They take on changing hues and shapes throughout the day as the sun moves. Even the moon silhouettes them differently against the night sky and sea. I read in my office: "Even though the mountains should move from their places and the hills fall into the sea, yet my love for you will stand firm."

Despite being the proud possessor of something called a "suitcase chapel", to translate from the Italian, bought in Rome, generally I do not find it easy to say Mass in a house or hotel, though it is something that is necessary when on holiday, especially if you're somewhere remote.

Here, however, it seems to be a kind of spiritual consolation all of its own. To look out on to so much beauty makes the heart spontaneously bless the God of all creation and offer him the fruits of the earth. I find the sense of awe with which one celebrates the Eucharistic sacrifice seems to resurge from deep within as at the end of a peaceful day.

I elevate the host to the silent praise of a beautiful world, and think of the words of the litany, "Heart of Jesus, desire of the eternal hills."

The tense sinews of the mind begin to relax. I sleep late and luxuriate in the total absence of any bleeps going, phones ringing, appointments to be kept or deadlines to be met, with the possible exception of getting my copy off to the Herald in time to take "Pastor Iuventus" into a fifth year in print.

The beauty of the natural world has a powerful effect on the weary spirit and I remember with a wry smile to myself the rather eccentric philosophy professor who used to make so much of "natural revelation" and St Paul's assertion to the Romans that anyone looking at the world around must be a fool if he cannot there discern evidence of the creator God.

I feel as if my spirit is soothed just by looking at the view. I have had a couple of days where I have just sat drinking it in, in between praying, reading and a sort of spiritual day-dreaming as I read a bit of Scripture and get a thought about something and that thought goes off at a tangent. And all the while the sky darkens and clears over the hills and sinking westwards blazons the purple of the heather on Hurlstone Point as it falls to the sea.

Then the twilight flattens all to monochrome and then to huge black silhouettes and the first lamp shines from a distant cottage and the first star appears. A crescent moon rises presently and I remembered with affection a youth I used to teach who told me that if you look long enough at such a moon you will eventually see all of it. He is absolutely correct and I have often had occasion to recall his advice. I wonder what he is doing now?

I get out for some long walks on the moor and through the great cathedrals of the woods while a strong breeze rustles a thousand trees on the hillside so that they shimmer silver and green. I visit the nearby villages and pop into the medieval churches with their characteristic squat towers and wagon vaults.

In one they are preparing for a flower festival; another is dedicated to St Dubricius, who was apparently a Welsh missionary (that's not a name one hears very often these days, but perhaps it's due for a comeback).

Just up the road from where I am staying there is a beautiful little chapel, which would only hold 10 or 15 people, and was once, long ago, the property of the monks of Athelney Abbey.

There's no avoiding the fact that these churches make me feel awkward; despite their being obviously well cared for. They have the feeling of waiting for something, the same feeling you get in a school during holiday time, or staying in a house belonging to someone who is away.

So the days pass in peace, which is what I need from this holiday more than anything else and have found in no small measure, thank God, this week. Like my friend looking at the moon, I needed the time to fix my gaze on God and at my own life at the moment, to look for signs of where he is revealing himself.

I need long enough to see if not the whole thing clearly at least the fact that there is a wholeness to it that even the shadow yields up, the more you look patiently and prayerfully.

Finding God in the spaces between

After Lourdes, and a few days at home with my family, I fly to Italy. The last time I came to Florence I was a student for the priesthood. Now, I am a priest. The feeling is like discovering an old photograph of yourself and realising, in a way that no longer impacts upon you from day to day, the extent to which you have changed.

Florence is such a beautiful city, despite the fact that it is more self-conscious than other Italian cities, and more expensive. Mind you, before we get on to matters aesthetical, I cannot get over how expensive Italy has become.

There is no question in my mind that the euro has been spectacularly inflationary; it is as if some prices were simply converted by removing the last three noughts and putting that little euro sign in front, so 3,000 lire became 3 euros, thereby more than doubling the prices.

I love the convent of San Marco, where Fra Angelico painted a fresco in every friar's cell. At the top of the stairs leading to the cells is his famous Annunciation.

It arrests one's gaze by the serenity it conveys. How can it do that? Ruskin said of him that he was not so much an artist, as an inspired saint. This is surely something more than technical mastery; the gentleness of the faces of the angel and Our Lady would melt the hardest heart. Two other things strike me forcibly about the picture. One is the distance that the angel is from Mary; each has a separate bay of the cloister, a pillar is between them. Today's imagery would surely want so intimate a conversation, so personal an invitation, to be delivered close up; within what the behavioural psychologists call the "intimate field" reserved for loved ones.

Yet the angel stands some distance away — if they both stretched their arms out their finger tips might just touch. The distance conveys to me something of the mystery that is involved in any encounter with God. It is not that I am to merge with the other — but contemplation of the other grows, as it were, in the space between us, and if I am to know the other, I must respect that space. There is something holy and mysterious there.

Though there is a distance, the angel's wings arch towards Mary, and her body and her head incline towards the angel. Above them, the arches of the cloister, in which the encounter takes place, also incline towards one another, reinforcing the gentle arcs that eventually meet. And this of course, is the other thing that strikes one forcibly.

To our eyes the picture looks old. It has that reassuring religious antiquity about it – it seems to come from a gentler, simpler past. Yet the setting is San Marco itself. It would have been an entirely contemporary setting for Fra Angelico's brethren – like the Jesuits having a picture of the Annunciation taking place in Farm Street church.

A corridor follows the square of the cloister and, on either side, the small cells of the friars, each one decorated with a masterpiece for contemplation, are now on show for a different kind of admiration; for San Marco is a museum.

Still, the pictures cannot fail to inspire reverence. They have something of the quality of icons about them, drawing the beholder into them. I have two favourites. One is the fresco of The Mocking of Christ in which Jesus sits blindfolded while disembodied hands slap him and strike him with a reed, and a mean face as it were suspended in midair spits at him. Its surrealism seems to be hundreds of years ahead of its time, but to such effect, for it shows what it is like to be blindfolded and to experience these outrages as disembodied, unidentifiable malignity.

The other I love is the Noli me Tangere. Here Fra Angelico has taken John's Gospel literally, and the risen Jesus appears as a gardener with a great spade over his shoulder.

As with the Annunciation, at the very centre of the picture is the space between the hand of Mary Magdalene reaching towards Jesus and his seeming to both reach towards her and indicate the space between them. The folds of Jesus' clothing incline towards Mary, even a fold or two caught by the wind and billowing towards her.

Perhaps this is the secret of the serenity and sweetness of these pictures: that they invite us to contemplation – to focus on a place in which we wait; we experience the space between desire and its fulfilment, between the invitation to intimacy and the freedom to respond.

September

Country life

I exchange the glories of Rome for the bucolic bliss of England's West Country and a few days of drinking in the peace. The cottage I have booked has views across the hills of Exmoor on one side and the North Devon Coast on t'other.

The scenery is a therapy in itself. Beauty always is, but there is a quality about this place which seems to calm and relax me and I have been wondering why exactly it should be such a haven. The scenery is rugged, after all; the hills like the shoulders of sleeping giants, the colours brown and green and purple and the wind catching the woods on Ley Hill like an unseen hand brushing the knap of a great green cloth.

St Paul says you can see the Creator in his works and here the scale and beauty of the place does raise the heart and mind, but in a way that leaves your feet rooted to the ground. To see the grandeur of God in this place leaves some deep, deep sense of belonging here; of being heir to this beauty that has formed over aeons of time.

So the routine is one of no routine: lazy mornings, farm eggs for breakfast and a leisurely read of the breviary, then maybe a walk. One day I take the path along the coast, on another trace the path that winds to the top of the beacon, another day's walk is through the ancient woodlands startling the occasional deer.

Sunday was particularly blissful. I know it is foolish, but somehow old habits die hard and though Sundays are now working days, something inside me still thinks of them with the habit formed from family and working life, as days of rest with a special feeling of sabbath. I am sure that this is no longer really the case for anyone now; so many shops are open and sports events take place. There is, of course, a great joy about Sunday still, but, at the risk of sounding petulant, I wish there was more time to enjoy it.

After Mass at the nearby parish this was the laziest Sunday I have had all year. How blissful to leave the lunch table with nothing more to occupy your thoughts than whether a bit of a walk or a bit of doze is more to the point. In the event I opted for a walk and a cream tea and I was curled up with a detective story just at the time when I would normally be girding my loins for the evening Mass.

It is so nice to forget what day of the week it is, so I can't tell you if it was Tuesday or Wednesday when I visited Cleeve Abbey. Cleeve was a Cistercian house with 16 or 17 monks when it was dissolved in 1537. The church is ruined, but the monastic buildings are the most completely preserved in England. There is a beautiful refectory intact, flooded with sunlight from the high lancet windows where the monks ate under the eyes of the carved angels who throng the roof. The upper floor of one whole wing of the cloister, some 50ft long, is the monks' dorter, or dormitory. The simplicity of the room is again picked out by the sun falling at regular intervals along the floor through the tall windows, as though a patch of golden light marked the space where each monk lay. They would have been up long before the sun, mind you, filing down the night stairs for Matins at 2.30am.

It is hard not to be irritated by some of the "educational" material provided by English Heritage who now own and manage the site. A display in the foyer glosses over the dissolution of the monasteries in a sentence, having pointed out that the Cistercians had begun a strict reform and, horror of horrors, by the sixteenth century had started to introduce some decoration into their churches, even some stained glass. Evidence of their corruption is again adverted to in the sacristy where there is "some colourful wall-painting". Likewise, we are supposed to be scandalised by the single fireplace in the monastery which was not provided for in the original rule. Add to this the fact that the monks' agricultural skills were such that they turned the poor land they had been given into flourishing farmland and it seems self-evident that something had to be done about them.

And so the house was closed and plundered and the monks pensioned off. Thus England lost her network of schools and social services for hundreds of years. More difficult to cost in terms of its damage, was the destruction of the monastic Opus Dei.

Here now the bare ruined choir stands where hills reach to heaven and the fields still need ploughing and reaping. Here still men live below the moor, troubled by the seasons of the heart and the frailty of love. No psalms ascend now in the valley, there is no one there to watch the night with prayer. Amidst so much beauty, somebody should be praising God for it, somebody raising heart and mind for all those whose gaze is bent down.

Back to work

It was hard to leave the beauty of Exmoor and the calm of the hills. The night before I left, the sky was clear and the stars were impossible to count and so close you felt if you climbed the beacon you might brush them with your outstretched hand. I thought of Abraham and the promise made him by God that his descendants would be as many as the stars of heaven.

As I contemplated, not without regret, another holiday ending, another year of routine beginning, I suddenly realised that God does not budget our happiness. It is not that he metes out happiness in days like holiday entitlement. If I could but live his will more fully, trust him more deeply, then joy would be unbounded. There is no end to what he wants to give us. His desire for our happiness is on a vast and profligate scale, like the stars.

Always you arrive back in the parish to a mountain of post, most of it completely uninteresting. On the answering machine there was a phone message from the son of a man whom I had visited in hospital about this time last year. He was the old soldier who seeing a priest in a pastoral stole with a pyx round his neck had somehow been reminded of a chaplain giving general absolution on the Normandy Beaches years before and he asked me to hear his confession. Then he had talked and talked about his part in the war, his life, how he had just quietly drifted from the Church. The son was calling to tell me that his father had died and asking me if I could celebrate his funeral. The message was two weeks old. I called the son nevertheless, who was very understanding and said that someone had told him I was away. His father had been buried without a Requiem Mass. He asked me if I would celebrate a Mass for him.

"He spoke very highly of you," the son said. We had corresponded a couple of times after he left the hospital for his home in a distant parish; he would write and ask me to say Mass for his dead wife. I remembered there was something very graced about our meeting – I wrote about it at the time. I hope that stayed with him in his last days. I have remembered him at Mass each day since.

On Monday morning I put my best foot forward and walking down the main road to the school I passed the house where Bridget used to live. She was one of my Wednesday morning ladies, I used to take her Holy Communion until her death aged 93 a couple of months ago. I saw the front door open and down the passage the door to her small studio flat beyond. It used to take her a full five minutes to struggle to open the door to me.

Now there was a builder pushing a barrow load of rubble out of the doorway of her flat. He looked quizzically at me. I couldn't really explain that I was thinking of Bridget with a mixture of sadness and happiness. It seemed sad to think that only now she was gone was the place being smartened up, presumably to be let at three times the rent. Wood floors and chromium fittings and minimalist décor would replace the colourful carpet and cosy clutter and express eloquently the different lifestyles and attitudes of the new and old owners. I felt strongly that Bridget, at peace in heaven, was beyond it all and wouldn't mind. But there was still something poignant about the transformation that was taking place.

I was rescued from my reverie by Bridget's neighbour returning from the shops. I had met Miriam at the funeral. I liked her very much. She was also a spinster, an ex-ballet dancer. She had the grace of movement that dancers embody. There was also something slightly fragile about her, a porcelain doll sort of beauty, but this was a demeanour, rather than something physical. She had the smile of someone who is used to being brave and positive in the face of adversity. She offered me a cup of coffee in her little flat, a mirror image of Bridget's and we chatted.

She reminisced about dance tours in Italy, told me about her Anglican parish and her work as a volunteer for the Red Cross. She spoke warmly of Bridget and her kindness, how Bridget had welcomed her when she first moved in.

I can imagine they got on well and that Miriam at least might still say a prayer for Bridget when the chromium and stripped pine bring their surgical reign to the little flat with the mulberry tree outside the window.

It is a shame that we see less easily how people are changed by one another, how the life and death of each one of us has an impact on everyone.

Coming to blows over the flowers

Last Sunday's Gospel parable of the labourers in the vineyard coincides with the end of the Trades Union Congress and a time when parish life is back to the heat of the noonday. There is a real sense of the year girding its loins and getting back to normal after the summer holidays. Each Monday evening I have what I call a "surgery" — a time when parishioners can call without appointment to discuss anything to do with parish life.

The attendance at the surgery is a useful barometer of parish life. Over the summer it was pretty slack. Now they are queuing round the corner – well, the corner of the lounge anyway. School applications are the real hot potato at this time of year. Every year I squirm with embarrassment as total strangers appear and swear on their granny's grave that they attend Mass every week and ask me to endorse a school application to that effect. Our church only holds about 150 people. I think it unlikely that I could have missed them for these past months, unless they were heavily disguised. I don't blame them at all for wanting to get their children into a decent school. I just object to their expectation that I ought to be a party to this deception.

Some cunning RE teacher sets an assignment which involves interviewing a parish priest, and so I have a string of bashful children and anxious parents wanting to put their list of questions to me about the church, or the parish, or what made me decide to be a priest. The latter is a complicated question which involves an answer which does not naturally flow at the speed of a 10-year-old's recording pencil, however hard I try to keep it simple. I notice that among my inspirations or reasons for being a Christian one child has dutifully written "the lies of the saints," and I start to fret about what else may have been transcribed wrongly.

The surgery can produce unusual encounters, such as the people who are convinced they are under curses, usually because something has happened for which they are quite clearly directly or indirectly responsible themselves, or the lady who seeks employment as a parish receptionist and who heads her list of qualifications by telling me she has just finished a course in salsa dancing, as though this will somehow clinch it. The church flower rota is proving a source of internecine strife at the moment, and I get people dropping in to denounce their fellow parishioners. I think that what every parish needs is a sort of independent commissioner for complaints, or a flower ombudsman who could adjudicate in such cases. I just want the flowers to look nice and am not therefore sufficiently alive to the subtler issues of flower politics. Other callers simply want Mass cards signed, or to book baptisms. One lady brought me a jar of home-made marmalade.

On Wednesday's Feast of the Exaltation of the Holy Cross we have a reunion of our deanery World Youth Day group. We have Mass followed by a fish and chip supper. It is a funny and very boisterous evening. I reflected how things had changed from the first meeting back in the early part of the year when there were awkward pauses and embarrassed silences. Now there is great laughter and shouting over photographs and a real sense of a group having been formed. I put two questions to them: How are we to build on what we had experienced? And, is it too early to start planning for Sydney 2008? The answer, to my delight, is that we should continue to meet monthly as we had before and that we should begin preparing for Sydney.

We have the quarterly finance committee meeting tonight. I have to explain to them why there is a sizeable discrepancy in what I said we would spend on improving the church and the excess we have spent. Perhaps I could tell them I am under a curse.

It occurs to me that the Feast of the Korean Martyrs is a good day to visit the pub across the road and welcome the new Korean owners. It has had a difficult history; the previous publicans arrived at the same time I did and only lasted 18 months. My desire to maintain good relations with the local pub is based on the worthiest of motives, you understand, a diplomatic mission to ensure that they understand how their karaoke could affect our evening Masses.

I pride myself on having good relations with all the local shops. The man in the convenience store calls me "mate"; the people in the fish and chip shop insisted on carrying the WYD fish and chips round for us the other night and gave us a free bottle of vinegar. The charming Hindu chemist asks me to bless sick customers, often to their consternation, and gives me helpful advice on treatment for my allergies. So there you have a picture of a bustling week here in our little community. St Mary Meade it ain't, but in the words of the hymn, it's new every morning.

Watching a soul slip away

September is the month for new starts. For example, it's generally when clergy moves happen. I was showing the new assistant priest from our neighbouring parish round the hospital last week. He will cover the times when I am not on-call. We were heading to get his photograph taken for his identity badge when a couple stopped me and asked me if I visited non-Catholics as well. The man's mother, it seems, was seriously ill, but not a Catholic, but his wife was Catholic and she had persuaded her husband that it would be a good idea for her to see the priest. They explained that other members of the family might not be so keen. I suggested that they go and discuss it with the rest of the family now, which would give me time to finish my tour and I would come up to the ward afterwards to see what they had decided as a family.

So we finished the tour, which provides a brief geography of the places to which the chaplain is likely to be called: A&E and the 'resus' room, and nearby the windowless room where they lay out the dead, with its connecting door to the patients' sitting room with its comfy sofas and pastel prints. We toured the high dependency unit, the critical care unit, the cardiac care unit, the labour ward and the special baby care unit where the premature babies are cared for in incubators.

We descended to the bowels of the hospital, to the communications centre where the ladies who staff the switchboard are ever cheerful and welcoming. They work long shifts themselves, but are always so kind, and will even apologise for disturbing you if they bleep you to summon you to an emergency at night.

The tour completed, I went up to the ward. I left my companion outside: one Catholic priest turning up if you are not sure you want him is one thing, two would be excessive. In the event, it seemed that all the family were happy for me to see their relative.

I bent over the frail figure in the bed and told her that I am the Catholic chaplain come to pray with her and give her the

Sacrament of the Sick. Her eyes opened and she seemed to take me in. She looked peaceful, not startled or anxious. I began praying and I anointed her, and gave her the Apostolic Pardon. Her eyes closed and I had just begun the Litany of the Saints when she slipped peacefully away, and I continued to say the prayer of commendation: "Go forth Christian soul."

"You know something," said her daughter, "she was waiting for that; she must have been waiting for you to get here," and she kissed me as though I were a member of the family.

I am very conscious that it is the time of year that our young people are going off to university. I have long thought it significant that this happens at the onset of autumn, and not say, in spring. I spoke to one mother after Mass this morning who said she had taken her daughter down to begin her university career at the weekend.

"She was alright, but I was in floods of tears," she laughed.

University is a time of almost unparalleled freedom, and yet that freedom itself is what defines it as the end of our childhood; we must learn to live with the responsibility of all that freedom.

"Please pray for her," the mother added. "She's reading theology and everyone says that's a sure way to lose your faith." And then she paused and said: "But she is strong in her faith." I thought that expressed beautifully the dilemma of a parent, whose reaction is to want to protect, and who, in fact, must stand back and trust their child to sound and be sounded by truth.

It may be bad enough letting your son or daughter go, but it's far worse for me, for I am losing most of my choir. Two years ago one exceptional sixth former formed some of his contemporaries into a choir, and now most of them are on their way to university. If I tell you that three of them are going to read music and the choirmaster has a choral scholarship to Cambridge you will get some idea of how talented they are, and what a loss they will be. More than that, they love singing good church music and have brought a real sense of mission to their work here that has been a huge support to me. As a priest, I still need to be inspired by the liturgy and moved and uplifted by it, and their music has often helped me.

I am very happy for their success, hugely grateful for what they have done for us here, full of hope for what they will become and what they will achieve as the Catholic musicians of the future, and find that all of those things mean I can be joyful or wistful about their going, even at the same time. They go with my blessing and prayers.

October

Baptism for a child born early

I was sorry, I have to say, that there were not more people there on Saturday to celebrate the Feast of the Archangels. It seems to me that devotion to the angels is one of those things which helps us keep an authentic perspective on what God is like in his beauty and majesty and holiness. They also remind us there is in our own lives a battle between the forces of darkness and light which we must join.

Saturday mornings are pretty much non-stop religion. We have novena, Mass, Confessions, exposition and Benediction until 11.30 for the usual faithful remnant. My Saturday afternoon routine is pretty static. It is the time for writing a sermon and putting the finishing touches to the newsletter. It always seems a short afternoon, with Confessions beginning just after five, and Sunday beginning with Mass at six. I was poring over the parable of the rich man and Lazarus and suddenly realising what a monster of selfishness Dives is, even in Hades, when the hospital bleep went.

I am called to the hospital's neo-natal unit. Here, babies born as early as 24 weeks – the legal time limit for abortion in this country, as if I needed to remind you – are given the intensive care which allows many of them to survive. More so even than elsewhere in the hospital, the neo-natal unit is a place of vertiginous highs and lows where life is all the more precious and miraculous for being tiny and frail, and all the more desperately fragile. It is a providence that the person in charge of it is a wonderful Irish Catholic woman whose dedication and compassion seem endless. Here is a case of someone really bringing the gospel to the world. What a force for good she is with her tireless devotion and her skills comforting and advising and just caring for the parents in this most anxious of situations. With the gentlest of touches she manages to steer any she feels are so disposed in the direction of the spiritual comfort the Church can provide.

Today I am asked to baptise a child born three months early and now 50 days old. This little mite has already doubled her birth weight of 600 grams, but she is still absolutely tiny. She has to undergo surgery on her heart if she is to survive and so the parents have asked for her to be baptised.

I meet them in a waiting room beforehand. In such moments in those featureless interview rooms by casualty units or intensive care wards I always think of T S Eliot's line "humankind cannot bear very much reality." Often because the shock of the situation makes it so hard to express feelings, conversation becomes strangely detached and general. The words are not very important; they are a way of trying to hold on to some sense of normality. Here today the parents, who are from Zimbabwe, launch into a long account of the reasons why they left and the political situation there and what they hear from the relatives and friends they have back home. The British Government and people do not know the half of what's going on, is in effect what they tell me.

We go into the intensive care unit and the mother is able to take the baby out of the incubator. The child is not more that eight or nine inches long, cradled in the crook of her mother's arm. Somehow the perfection of the human form in miniature like this makes it even more staggering; the tiny hands and fingernails, the delicate ears, the eye lashes on the little brown eyes which open and stare unfocused for a few seconds. I feel clumsy and huge and ungainly stooping over her to sign her with the sign of the cross. I trickle a few drops of water on the tiny head and by this simple sign claim her for the new life of the resurrection won for us by Mary's child.

And suddenly in this place of sterile cleanliness and state-of-the-art medical equipment the scent of the oil of Chrism fills the air as I anoint the tiny head. The strange perfume wafts into this place of twenty-first century technology the memory of an ancient salvation. Thus it would have been when Samuel anointed the boy David, when Solomon was crowned, and thus in the eternity of his love still more ancient and more new, God chose this child, chose her in Christ before she was born.

And I want to weep, not because it is sad she is ill or because there is a poetic beauty in the rite, but because I am convinced it is true; it is God's choice of her which is the only thing which matters. Outside of this truth nothing else does really matter and yet I am conscious that I am so often living as though it did; that seems suddenly so wearying and shabby.

At the heart of human existence is not the race against death to find meaning, but the indestructible force of this love coming closer and closer towards us, for us to recognise it and embrace it. To do so we must become like little children.

The Mass maketh the man

Outside my bedroom window the golden leaves of autumn tell their own story about how time has passed and how long I have been here now. By the church wall there is the most beautiful holly tree. It is covered with scarlet berries, presaging a hard winter. And so the world rolls on, and life seems busier than ever with hospital visits, school Masses, deanery meetings, finance committee meetings, Confirmation and First Communion courses.

I have had an interesting experience this week. The local Catholic school, as part of the RE syllabus for Year Sevens (that's to say 11 year olds just starting at secondary school), have set the children a project on their parish church and their parish priest.

This is a clever piece of work. It has produced numbers of Catholics whom we would otherwise not see and at least brought them into contact with their parish church. I have answered the same questions many times. How long have you been a priest? Did you do anything before? When was the church built? What is its history?

The pupils are interested to hear that the church is so relatively young, and the story of the dynamic Monsignor whose pastoral care, empire-building zeal and rivalry with the next door parish combinedly drove him to build our little church to be a chapel of ease. (It was said of him that he was so convinced he would be made a bishop that he had all the episcopal regalia ready in a bottom drawer. It's a good story, even if it's not true, but not one I would repeat to my Year Seven inquirers.) I show them the chalice and ciborium engraved with his family name, and the original vestments, now somewhat worn, but obviously costly and of the highest quality, even for so modest a church. He never did become a bishop.

Gerard Manley Hopkins wrote rapturously about "all trades, their gear and tackle and trim" and there is something about the specialist equipment for anything that cannot fail to be interesting. This is true of the church and the sacristy. To show the .

young people the safe with the silverware, the oil stocks and the monstrance, the marriage registers, and the sacristy cupboards with their vestments and linen and candles is a great catechetical opportunity and the children are genuinely fascinated by them. The pièce de résistance is the display of relics and the skull-cap of a long dead pontiff – undoubtedly quality grist to the project-writer's mill.

Then comes the question, "What do you do apart from say Mass?" There is behind the enquiry an interesting mind-set, a correct one that defines a priest in terms of his sacramental function. A priest is first and foremost someone who offers sacrifice. Beyond this essential their understanding is vague. It is a question that people quite frequently ask. The temptation is to expostulate that this is only a tiny part of what a priest does, for so it is in terms of the time taken. And yet the perception behind it is a vital one. I wonder have I made the same connection myself deeply enough, namely that everything I say and do in some way is supposed to be connected with standing at the altar day by day? Saying Mass is not just something I fit into a working day; it is the reason for all the work. I remember how since childhood I have said the morning offering I was taught at school: "O Jesus ... I offer you all my prayers, works, sufferings and joys for all the intentions of thy Divine Heart in the most Holy Mass."

After a pause for this somewhat abstract reflection, I try to enumerate the other things I have done this week. I have prepared next year's budget for the parish finance committee to approve. I have visited the hospital five out of the seven days. I have written school references, seen to the banking, done wedding preparation, baptism preparation, two Masses in different schools, worked on our proposed deanery pilgrimage to the World Youth Day, prepared things for Confirmation and First Holy Communion classes, as well as thinking about November lists, Christmas cards, household insurance and doing my own tax return (still unfinished).

But the Year Seven project, if nothing else, has reminded me of this important lesson: that my real task as a priest is to connect all this activity with the still centre of the turning circle, the Mass.

To the extent that I do this – that this one function is the fulcrum on which everything else turns – everything else will be graced, and the offering of the Mass will transform them as it transforms the everyday gifts of bread and wine.

Bearing new life in my hands

No sooner is the new surgical wing not quite finished than they are building again at the hospital – this time a new cancer wing. The only tangible result of the new construction to date is that the already inadequate provision for car parking is further reduced and there is a new entrance where the exit used to be. This has already involved me in two near-crashes as someone blithely drives out of what they still believe to be the exit just as I am turning into what is designated the new entrance. I had resolved to walk to the hospital to avoid these problems but the frequency and urgency of calls always seems to end up defeating my resolution. In fact, as time goes on, so the relentless nature of the hospital chaplaincy seems to defeat more and more good resolutions.

Late on Saturday night I was called to a patient who had already died. The frequency with which this happens is evidence of a growing need for catechesis on the Sacrament of the Sick and what we actually mean by Last Rites. I go and say prayers over the body. There are 27 people standing round the bed in the ward, all squeezed within the curtains.

Early on Sunday morning came an alarm call from the hospital's maternity suite. My heart sank. Of all the tasks which fall to a hospital chaplain surely the most demanding is going to see parents who have lost their babies. So it was a huge relief to be told that this time the summons was not to some tragedy, but to a new mother who wanted Holy Communion. I arrived on the ward after Mass and found the mother looking very tired, just trying to doze. In a crib next to her, just peeping out from under his wraps, was an adorable little baby boy. He was fast asleep. It was no mere flattery to tell his proud mother that he really was beautiful. I gave her Holy Communion and we thanked God for the gift of her child, her second, whose tiny head I signed with the cross as he lay there.

As I was packing up my things to go the baby stirred and began to cry a little. "Could you pass him to me?" the mother asked. "It's very awkward for me." Her bed was low and she was doubtless recovering from her confinement. It was a natural thing to ask, but I was rather taken aback all the same. Ever so carefully I lifted the little boy, being careful to put my hand under his head, and handed her the precious bundle. It was a moment of rare joy in a place where so often one has to stiffen the sinews to bear distress and even physical revulsion at what one is seeing. It was but a moment, yet the touch of that precious life was somehow healing. It made me realise how easy it is to disconnect in some way from the scenes to which one is called, how often there is a temptation to disengage in order to deal with one's own feelings.

As the day wore on I was conscious of all kinds of thoughts and feelings stirred by this most simple of requests. One of them centres on the juxtaposition of the actions of putting first the Blessed Sacrament and then shortly afterwards her child into the mother's hands.

When something is small and infinitely precious it is easy, if you are not used to it, to be frightened of its preciousness, or rather of one's own clumsiness or unfamiliarity with something so vulnerable. This in turn can make one more clumsy, more lacking in dexterity. Babies need the sure grip of love, not the reverent touch of the connoisseur. Jesus makes himself vulnerable in the Blessed Sacrament not so that we can be all uptight and precious about it, but so that we can love him. The fear of making a mistake, of not being able to cope with his preciousness, can actually create a block to loving him – which is a crude definition of scrupulosity.

When taking the Blessed Sacrament in my hands I need to guard against any casual approach but also against what I might call Idealism. True reverence can only come from touching the reality of holiness, not from being frightened to touch it lest one's clumsiness and unfamiliarity betray one. When I speak of the sacramental body of Christ I am speaking about a mystery to be grasped with love, a beating heart put into these clumsy, awkward hands, so that they may learn how to love and care by experience of what they handle. Only in touching do they learn not to fear its fragility but to treasure it as token of the infinite life embodied in this precious thing. Thus touch becomes not a fearful self-awareness of responsibility but an instinctual, sure cradling of love for one precious and beautiful.

Young Winston

No sooner have I ceased waxing lyrical, or what you will, about how it's all back to routine than I am asked to bless my first polo pony. That is to say, I bless a polo pony for the first, and for all I know, the last time.

A very well-spoken young woman telephoned me and asked me with great charm if I would come and bless her polo pony. She wasn't a parishioner, and on inquiring why I had been chosen for this honour she said matter-of-factly that she drove past our church on the way to the polo club and had taken the number down.

I duly turned up at the polo club some six miles distant on Tuesday morning with a sense of slight unreality and a nagging doubt as to whether I needed the permission of the parish priest to bless a pony within his boundaries. I drove down a long driveway and came to a large flat, dusty field. The striped goal posts and rectangular divisions proclaimed even to my unpractised eye that this must be where they played polo. There were some rather ramshackle looking sheds round about and a sort of marquee affair, so I drove on looking for a club house or something more substantial by way of evidence of human habitation. All I found was another, similar field so I drove back to where I came in, stirring up huge clouds of dust as I went. There waiting for me was the young lady. I stopped the car and we introduced ourselves at the side of the enormous polo field. She told me she would tell the groom to fetch the ponies, plural.

It transpired that Winston was the only one to be blessed, but he had a stable-mate and it seems they did everything together, so the other, whose name I have forgotten because it was more exotic than Winston, had to come and watch though he was already blessed. "By the way," she added, "do you speak Spanish or Italian? You see, the grooms are all from the Argentine and don't understand English." (Most polo ponies, I discovered, are from the Argentine too, but from the way she later spoke to Winston it seems they pick English up faster.)

In a few minutes the ponies appeared, coming out of the sun, the Argentinean groom riding one bareback and leading the other on a rope attached to his head collar. As they stirred up the dust it was reminiscent of a scene from High Chaparral; well perhaps High Chaparral meets 'Brideshead Revisited' and 'Monsignor Quixote'. They were truly noble creatures. Polo ponies are thoroughbred racehorses crossed with smaller animals to produce a beast which is capable of great speed but can also stop suddenly and turn on a sixpence. These were sleek and muscled, but with the gentleness that comes from great strength tamed.

I put on a stole and began the blessing. The groom and the young lady crossed themselves and stood heads bowed in prayer. I had the pocket ritual with me which contained a blessing for flocks and herds that with some grammatical changes could be adapted to the blessing of a polo pony. I had given some thought as to an appropriate piece of scripture, and sifted through the psalms. After rejecting "Some put their trust in horses, but we in the name of the Lord," and "Be not like horse and mule, unintelligent, needing bridle and bit," both of which seemed a bit pointed, I settled for "The eyes of all creatures look to you O Lord and you give them their food in due season," which turned out to be nothing if not prophetic. I blessed the pony with some holy water at which he shied slightly, but our ceremony was soon over.

The young lady was very pleased and felt, she told me, so much happier now Winston was blessed. She dashed to her car and came back with a camera, a present wrapped and beribboned, a card and a bottle of pink champagne. I was on the point of saying, "Oh, you really shouldn't have!" when she presented all three to Winston for inspection. It seems they were for him. The card she opened; it felicitated him on the occasion of his blessing. The box contained Belgian chocolates which Winston generously shared with us, as he did the champagne. We drank out of plastic cups, the ponies snorted it out of plastic bowls. Luckily they didn't like pink champagne as much as the ordinary kind so there was more for us. After this I was given a tour of the stables and a standing invitation to watch polo any time I liked. I left totally charmed by the whole experience. I can't wait to see the photographs in Tatler!

November

The saints in light

Reading the scriptures for the Feast of All Saints there are two images which stay with me.

One is a memory from childhood. It was a year when there were power cuts; perhaps it was the year of the miners' strike of 1974. If you remember, what used to happen was first the lights would go off for a couple of seconds and then come on again. You knew that meant you would be plunged into darkness in about twenty minutes. We were in church for an evening Mass of All Saints, a huge cathedral of high vaults and deep chapels. The warning came and the church was in blackness for a few moments and then the light came on again. There was a sense of inevitability about what would happen next; I was waiting for the darkness to return, for then I was afraid of the dark. But I need not have feared. Some twenty minutes later when the lights went off the church was full of candles; hundreds, maybe thousands of them on candle stands and branched candlesticks and on every balcony and in every niche. The dreaded darkness was tamed; no longer terrifying, it was pierced by a thousand friendly lights.

In some way I have always connected this with the picture given us in the readings for All Saints; the image of a huge crowd. St John speaks of the vast crowd, impossible to count in his Apocalypse – a word which means lifting the veil; or if you like, seeing into the darkness. A crowd of people from every race joining with the angels in a huge surge of joy and love which emerges as one voice, millions strong: "Victory to our God who sits on the throne and to the Lamb." Anyone who has ever been to a football match or a Papal Mass like the ones in Rome will know what a powerful feeling it is to be part of a huge crowd.

Who is in this particular crowd? The crowd in the Gospel listening to the Sermon on the Mount gives us a clue: the poor in spirit, the gentle, the merciful, peacemakers, lovers of justice. It is a crowd of ordinary people who have endured their share of suffering, of great persecution. There are no also-rans here. They have triumphed over the big and little traumas of life by walking with God, their hand in his. They came through life trusting that there is a power, a love that lies like hidden gold in the dross of mourning and calumny and persecution; that shines out with value when held up in the light of Heaven.

Imagine how it will be, meeting all these people who know our hopes and sorrows and joys, who look on not merely as spectators, but with sympathy and help. For they help us, the members of the Church Triumphant. They have come through the great persecution and like those who have suffered much they have a deep solidarity with those who are still facing similar things.

In this crowd there will be no strangers. "There will be no such thing as an indifferent glance in heaven," says St Thérèse of Lisieux. We will be welcomed, please God by all our loved family and friends and more, by people we never knew cared for us, people who we suddenly see were quietly praying for us is life, or doing us unknown, unremembered acts of kindness. We will be welcomed by people we never knew in this life, but who have watched us from Heaven with eyes of full love.

I like to ponder too the thought that Heaven will see the perfection of all our relationships which now are wounded by sin. All Saints is perhaps the ideal Feast on which consciously to bring into the sight of God all the broken relationships we have known, not merely past ones severed by death, but the present ones soured by misunderstanding and mistakes, all those family feuds, those friendships soured, all those unrequited loves. When we meet these people in Heaven these ties too will be healed and whole. For there are only the meek and the gentle and those interested in making peace; those who hunger for justice. It will be the perfection of our relationships now. Our poor efforts to live the Beatitudes will be completed by grace, our potential realised. Heaven is not a separate existence, but the end of our pilgrimage; distant, but calling us with its grandeur, its beauty.

The Saints are not impossibly remote but near. If we would achieve our pilgrimage we must journey awhile in the unlit, hidden ways of meekness and peacemaking, hunger for justice, purity of heart. We will find that here it is not darkness at all, but a host of welcoming lights as the saints point the way to eternal Light.

On death and dying

A long, slow march through the cemetery saying the rosary. Today, the Sunday after All Souls, we always have a service for the Faithful Departed. The rhythm of prayer and the crunch of feet on the path lie gently on the uncanny stillness of the place. They seem to belong, like the birdsong and the wind in the trees. It is scarcely possible to believe that we are in the middle of a city. It is not actually raining, but there is a dampness in the air which begins to soak through the clothes and shoes. The sun will set in less than an hour, and already the grey skies are turning leaden.

I find myself admiring the monuments and the well-clipped yews, and realise that I am echoing a mantra of my great aunts who were forever speaking of cemeteries as though they were municipal parks or golf courses, commenting on how well they were kept or denouncing the iniquity of owners who didn't keep them looking nice.

We pause by the grave of a former parish priest. He died the year I was born. The current parish priest leads the prayer and then blesses the grave of his predecessor with holy water. The graves all about are buried in fallen leaves the colour of saffron; there is a sympathetic quality about them, as though the world weeps with us. "It is the blight man was born for ... that you mourn for," says Hopkins, to one who mourns the falling of the leaves. Perhaps this is what makes us feel so far from the city. It is not just that we are geographically separated; we are far from the noise and activity of living, where toil and worry allow us to forget that this is where we will end up.

In the city death has become the only taboo. I come here myself often in my "professional" capacity, but I suspect that what this place means has little impact on the consciousness of many who live within its catchment.

I have been reading Elizabeth Kubler-Ross's 'Living with Death and Dying', a sequel to her seminal work, 'On Death and Dying', which examines the psychology of coming to terms with death. She says that none of us believes in our own death. It is an interesting thought and one that I suspect is true enough for many of us. Try it. Ask yourself if you believe it. If you are like me there is a momentary acceptance of the notion that I must one day die but I regard it as so remote, so distant as to have no effect now. It's like saying I believe I will one day be old and grey and be unable to do the things I can do now. I have no real belief that this is so beyond a lot of words whose meaning I have yet to identify for myself.

Kubler-Ross says something else very interesting, which is that as children we have no fear of death. Writing movingly on her work with dying children she says that adults are the ones who make this transition difficult by their evasions and inability to deal with "unfinished business".

We are born, she says, fearful of only two things: loud noises and falling. All other fears we learn. It is thought-provoking.

No, you only dwell on death if you have business here at the cemetery. I know of parishioners, newly bereaved, who come here most Sundays and whose Christmas Day would be incomplete without a visit to their loved ones' graves.

They have a point. The psalmist says, "With you there is mercy and fullness of redemption", and their sad visits here to mourn and tend graves are an expression of the hope for a fullness of redemption. They know, by faith, that the souls of their departed live on in God, but they also know that other article of faith, that they await a bodily resurrection, a fullness of redemption.

At funerals there is a danger that we speak of immortality of the soul in such terms as to suggest that bodily death is a sort of sleight of hand. (How often people want to read the well-meaning verse which begins "Death is nothing at all … I have only slipped away into the next room.") But we are not Platonists or Hindus. The human person is soul and body; it is the both that make us who we are. We have no pre-existent soul; it is a new act of God's creation at our conception. It is not that we once dwelt in Heaven and are exiled. Heaven beckoned from our first moments as a living being and Heaven must encompass all that we are and have been but for sin. This is why as Catholics we profess the doctrine of the Assumption, why we venerate relics, and why there are times we feel it is good and salutary to visit the cemetery.

A Time For Healing

As I sit here and write, the sound of a saxophone comes drifting from the direction of the convent, but that must be the wind paying tricks; surely it's coming from the school? I celebrated the ten o'clock Mass this morning. And after you've lingered and chatted a bit and had a cup of coffee there is not really a lot of the morning left by the time you sit down to your desk.

There's nothing but rubbish and bills in the post and my desk is soon cleared; well, clearer. There's a sort of limbo area for things not important enough to file and not sufficiently trashy to chuck. Some of these papers might just have greatness thrust upon them should some circumstances make them suddenly topical. Others I might get round to reading should the news come through that hell has frozen over.

Time is a great healer. Once a month or so I sift through this pile and discover that most of it is totally out of date and can be jettisoned. In many respects all this is starting to sound like a conceptual artist's portrait of my mind, so let's press on swiftly.

At one o'clock sharp the gong announces a huge presbytery lunch of meat and about twenty-seven vegetables followed by steamed pudding and custard. At least I will walk some of it off down the dingy hospital corridors this afternoon.

However hard you try, you end up going everywhere twice when you find that patients have been moved from ITU to the ward you've just visited, or vice-versa, but I shouldn't complain. Our local hospital is much better than the others. I can still go to the receptionist for a computerised list of the Catholic patients. The other hospitals will no longer do so, on the basis that it is an infringement of a patient's rights to give out personal information.

How we would operate without it, I really don't know. We would pick up the local, practising Catholics whose friends or relatives had told us they were in hospital, but we would miss so many like those who came from further away. Today, for example, I see a man who has come from Malta for some very specialised operation.

We would miss those who are lapsed but for whom the experience of illness and hospitalisation is a warning that calls them back to their faith. We would also miss those who are lonely and housebound.

I met such a man today and it was a beautiful encounter. This man looked very ill, greeted me very warmly and explained that his mobility was such that he couldn't get to Mass very often. He knew the name of his church and his parish priest, which is always a good sign. He told me he had to have an operation on his spine. I never ask what they are in hospital for. Most will tell you anyway, and if they don't, they don't want to talk about it. I gave him the Sacrament of the Sick, and Holy Communion which he received with great devotion. As we finished his eyes filled with tears and he asked if we could say a prayer for his wife who died some twenty years ago.

Now one might say that it is natural for him to be feeling lonely and vulnerable and so he weeps for his wife, but I am sure there is something more going on.

The grace of the sacraments unlocks memories for healing, for suddenly our whole lives are open to the love of God. The sacraments come to us at a particular time in our lives, placing us in the presence of the eternal God. All that we have been and suffered is there for Him to love and heal when we receive Him in Holy Communion.

The ritual too, which accompanies us throughout our lives acts on our memories and can open them to healing. Seeing my two-sided pastoral stole of white and purple, the man tells me how he remembers receiving absolution from a chaplain on a battlefield in Normandy in 1944.

The padre invited all the troops, not just the Catholics, but anyone who "Wanted to say a little prayer", to come aside for a moment, and he gave them all absolution before they pressed on into the thick of battle. His eyes are once more full of tears as he tells me this, and then says that there are times now when he feels very afraid; he particularly worries that he will be alone and unable to summon help if something terrible happens.

He apologises for his "unmanly" show of grief, but I tell him that the tears are a sign of healing. "I can't tell you what a comfort your visit has been to me," he says. But after all, I have done nothing more than my duty.

We will meet again in heaven

This will make very distressing reading, I'm afraid. I hesitate to write about so painful a subject matter for fear of upsetting people, but something in me feels compelled to write about it. Not only is there a kind of therapy in sharing it, but more, I think that what I experienced has the most profound implications. These are the kind of details the "pro-choice" lobby does not want anyone to know. They would dismiss them as "emotive" arguments. You will be able to judge whether their force is merely emotional or not.

The hospital bleeper went and I was called to a ward which I know is the ward where they perform what they call "terminations". It is hidden away in a basement. I discovered it, and its purpose, by hazard. It was not shown me or even mentioned when I was taken on a tour of the hospital. I have worked out its purpose by a rather sad process of deduction. I have been called twice to women who tell me they have had a "routine operation" that went badly wrong, leaving them with complications. I deduced the ward's purpose from the attitude of the nurses who, in contrast to everywhere else, seem suspicious of me and tight-lipped when I appear. Here they keep me waiting and say they must check to see that I have indeed been called in to see a patient.

I was called to bless the remains of a baby born at 16 weeks. I do not know for sure whether the baby miscarried or there was an intervention, but the parents wanted neither to see me nor to be present at the blessing. I have done several such blessings, in similar circumstances, and I now think that it is possible that these poor parents, suddenly realising the implications of this "routine operation", feel the need to mark the passing of their child somehow. Whatever is the case, no one who saw what I did could be under any illusion that this child of 16 weeks gestation was a child, a human person.

The nurse took me into an office and asked me to wait. She returned shortly, bringing in a small plastic bucket with a lid and asked me if I wanted the lid on or off. I said I wanted it off, naturally. I think that was the most tragic part of it all, really, seeing the bucket. She left me. In the bucket was a tiny, perfect child. A human child, the most innocent, vulnerable looking thing you could imagine. I tried to pray, and I blessed this tiny body with holy water and said Psalm 139: "O Lord, you search me and you know me, for it was you who created me, knit me together in my mother's womb ... I thank you for the wonder of my being." I read the Gospel about Jesus laying his hands on the little children. I uttered these words of faith in the oldest, Jewish sense of that word, meaning that this is the ground I am standing on, that this child is known to God, held by Jesus.

I do not in any way "understand" or perceive why this tragedy should happen, but I trust that there is a Love that can give even this meaning. And to that Love I cry in the name of the little child, and in my own name, overwhelmed by the horror of it.

Suddenly, looking down at this little child, I was gifted with a certainty that I would see the child in heaven. I cannot really describe the feeling I had of a connection with this child. In the abominable desolation of that office and that atmosphere I wept, because I felt sure I would encounter this person in heaven and all would be healed. I cannot explain it more.

Any sense of revulsion or squeamishness at what I was seeing left me and I felt a strange peace. How could God not receive such innocence into his Kingdom? I know we are bound by the sacraments, but he is not. Surely there is a baptism of desire, or indeed of blood, for these poor, little ones who witness to the sacredness of human life, which is itself a witness to its Creator and Redeemer?

I tried to make myself look presentable and professional and left the office. Now I wonder why I did. Perhaps it was a mistake.

Later in the week I was called to a woman who had been told the baby she was carrying had died. Her devastating grief was multiplied because the baby had died as a result of an amniocentesis test that had gone wrong.

"Why did I agree to have the test?" she kept crying. "It's not as if I would have done anything, even if they had detected any abnormality. Why did I say yes?"

Six hours later, she had delivered the child and I went back to bless the little body. She was cuddling it and crying.

Providence decreed that later the same day I would see my own newborn niece, Marthe Maria, healthy and beautiful. Her birth seems even more of a miracle and a blessing as a result of what I now know, in other circumstances, might have been.

December

Do they know it's Advent?

Advent has begun and is already being routinely trounced as a season in its own right. Curiously, from what I have seen, the shops seem to have been more restrained this year, and have held back with the full Christmas drive and the "White Christmas" tapes until an almost indecently late November. By contrast some Catholic institutions seem to have moved things even further forward and I am already aware of carol services and nativity plays that will be done and dusted before the second Sunday of Advent. There is the risk of appearing pompous and holier than thou if you suggest that you are not ready to sing Christmas carols in the first week of December. We don't sing "Christ the Lord is Risen today", on the third Sunday of Lent so why should Christmas be different? I know, I go on about this every year. I will get myself a sandwich board and walk up and down the high street proclaiming, "The beginning is nigh", or else release a pop song called "Do they know it's Advent?" It seems to me such a wonderful season of grace that it's too good to miss. I also happen to find Christmas all the more enjoyable for not running out of momentum by Boxing Day. My sandwich board will advertise prizes for anyone who has managed to find a Christmas carol service or concert that takes place in Christmastide.

The beautiful strains of the Rorate Caeli sound the sober joy of the liturgy of the first Sunday of Advent. St Mark's Gospel has a starkness about it, as Jesus urges everyone repeatedly to stay awake as you do not know the hour of the master's return. I think from now on it will always conjure up a particular scene for me. I was going round the hospital with Holy Communion on Saturday evening and woke one poor lady from a deep drug-induced slumber to read that Gospel and give her Holy Communion. She smiled so sweetly and was able to stay awake just long enough to receive a small fraction of the Sacred Host before drifting away again. She was very poorly. I have a feeling it may turn out to be her last Communion, her Viaticum, food for her final journey. This must have been at about the same time as the Holy Father was addressing the faithful at Vespers in St Peter's on the meaning of Advent. "God calls us to communion with him," he said, "and that communion will be fully realised with the return of Christ, and he himself undertakes to ensure that we are ready when we reach this final and decisive encounter."

Before the evening Mass I baptised another little Filipino baby, the second I have baptised from the same family in the 18 months I have been here. The Filipino community are a source of great joy and hope; they are such wonderful witnesses to the value of family life. A very beautiful Advent wreath stands ready and waiting for a single candle to be lit and I suppose I was more aware of it than ever because of the Filipino custom of having all the many godparents holding a lighted candle and standing round the baby like a sort of human wreath. Perhaps because of that the prayer which accompanies the giving of the baptismal candle struck me with renewed emphasis today: "May he keep the flame of faith alive in his heart, when the Lord comes may he go out to meet him with all the saints in the heavenly kingdom." It seems to confirm that idea of Pope John Paul's about the "Advent structure" of our faith. We have the flame of faith already in our heart through baptism, and it is there for us to tend so that we may go out and meet the Lord who comes.

In Rome, the Holy Father was saying: "The future is, so to say, contained in the present, or better still in the presence of God himself, in his indefectible love which ... does not abandon us for a moment, just as fathers and mothers never cease to follow their children's development."

Advent, then, is a journey which parallels that of our whole life – a journey carrying that flame to meet the Lord, a journey of sanctification.

"Faced with Christ who approaches, Man feels called with all his being. Sanctification is a gift from God, it is his initiative, but human beings are called to correspond to that with all their being, leaving nothing of themselves excluded," Pope Benedict explained.

It is in all those parts of my being where Christ is excluded through fear or sin or neglect or some consequence of my personality or history that salvation will blossom, there that he will tear the heavens to come down.

I don't know about you, but I need time and space to become more aware of those, consciously to go out to meet him in these unlikely places. This is the particular task and joy of Advent, but I'd never get all that on my sandwich board.

The knees of my heart shall I bow ...

I have been conducting an experiment into the collective memory of the Christian population. You can do it yourself. If you want an insight into your friends' past bring up the subject of the school nativity play. It will reveal some of the earliest and most formative of childhood memories.

Everyone I ask seems to have been in a nativity play and all have strong memories of them. I myself was St Joseph. I wore my dressing gown back to front, and a tea-towel headdress. Interestingly enough, though that is very vividly implanted in my mind, I have no recollection whatsoever of any other detail of the play or cast. I just remember feeling it was something of an indignity to be seen in public with your nightwear on backwards.

I suppose any serious sociological study ought to try to make some connection between what a person's role was in the nativity play and how they turned out in later life. That might take more time than I have on hand at the moment. Do those beautiful angels with their tinsel haloes take on something of the personage as well as the role? Do the little fellows in the woolly sheep's heads end up being easily led, the innkeepers go into service industries?

One of the nice things about being in a parish which contains high numbers of aspirational parents is that the costumes for the nativity plays are of sumptuous quality. In the school hall the children are being marshalled for their journey to Bethlehem via the church.

Amongst the folk making their way to the stable this year is a delegation of Victorian folk, the boys dressed as chimney sweeps and Artful Dodgers, the girls in crinolines and mob caps and in some cases what look like granny's pearls. It is a curious thing, but somehow in costume you always see the person shining through more directly; as if to dress in strange clothes is to frame the personality in a way that makes it stand out more. One really does see the children in a transformed light. And I reflect that the noun "person" was originally a theological term for speaking about the threefold life of the Trinity. It came from the word for the masks the actors wore through which they spoke their lines.

Unusually on such occasions, the church is hushed save for a gentle rustling of proud parents. Two children play the Bach/Gounod Ave Maria on piano and viola and the lights are dimmed. Slowly, in comes the procession of shepherds and sheep and angels and wise men and sweeps all carrying candles. The costumes and the children's faces shown only in the candlelight suddenly take on a timeless, iconic quality. Here is the world of childhood, beautiful, open, graced, and as we know all too well, vulnerable. And suddenly I hear the familiar story unfold with a new joy; ravished by the sheer beauty of it; the mystery of the great and holy both revealed and veiled in the beauty of a tiny child. The vast Creator who "deigns to be ... on Joseph's arm or Mary's knee." God in the simple and hidden, God making himself vulnerable.

It is also possible to see reflected in the candlelit faces of the children, the fact that humanity does have a natural beauty about it. It was after all made "very good", made with the thought that Christ would share this nature. When God fashioned the face of Adam He thought first of the One who was to come.

"Christian be aware of your dignity," Pope Leo says in his Christmas sermon. The dignity of the little child who plays Mary or Joseph brings tears to our eyes because it is the dignity and beauty in each of us; each cast a starring role in this story of God coming to us if we can but accept it. That is where children have the edge on us.

Soon the familiar story comes to its climax and by now the altar is covered with angels and kings and sheep and the gentiles from all different centuries. I have to start doing my bouncer's act and restraining over-eager parents anxious to capture this moment forever in the virtual reality of a video. To my mind it is the very ephemerality of it which makes it beautiful and even if it isn't you can't behave like that in church anyway.

We conclude with some prayers; good ones. "Christmas is about giving. Without giving there is no Christmas; without sacrifice there is no true worship." Someone here has thought very carefully about this.

But the image I will treasure this Christmas was of the child Mary. She left the scene last and as she did so, carrying her doll Christ-child, with the unselfconsciousness of habit, turned and genuflected reverently to the tabernacle. And I thought of the words of the medieval carol, "The knees of my heart shall I bow."

God is with us.

Awaking to the light of Christ
(December 24)

There is a certain amount of surprise in the parish when I schedule Midnight Mass for midnight. It seems that in previous years there has been trouble from late-night revellers from the pub opposite and so "Midnight Mass" has been moved to before closing time. I have decided to take a more defiant approach. First I thought of hiring a couple of security guards from a private firm. As well as being rather costly, I don't know that this is the right tone to set. We need to differentiate, I feel, between peaceable drunks who are drawn by remembrance or hope, albeit in a sentimental or confused way, whose presence is to be welcomed, and those merely bent on causing trouble. In my youth I clearly remember hefty sidesmen summarily ejecting troublemakers from Midnight Mass with a heave and a "Happy Christmas". Somehow they could do so because a certain deference, a residual awe about being in church, made even the drunks reluctant to push their luck. In a society in which, according to a recent survey, one in three people do not know that Jesus was born in Bethlehem, it is unlikely that such awe can be taken for granted now. The sidesmen seem older and frailer these days, and are doubtless far more anxious about the possibility of finding themselves charged with assault or worse.

I decide, therefore, to consult the local police for some advice. I get an operator and then an interminable wait with a recorded message which repeats often enough for me to order some carol sheets, send three e-mails and pay my credit card bill using the other line before finally connecting with a real live person. When I do, they are very helpful and once we have got over the usual problem of explaining that I am not St Onesimus, merely his parish priest, the officer finally locates us on the computer and promises to send a presence to the vicinity to keep watch over my flock by night. I get a reference number, presumably to quote at any would-be troublemakers, since it begins with the acronymn CAD.

A few days, or rather nights, before Christmas Eve the bleeper summons me to the hospital and a death in the early hours of the morning. Woken suddenly from deep sleep, and conscious of the need for haste, the mind goes into a kind of overdrive in which it does routine things like dressing almost unconsciously, while some part of it wanders as though still dreaming. In this state I go into the office to find my sick call set and my ritual. I am suddenly startled; for the room appears to be full of small people. In fact it is the crib figures, there for safety till the crib is ready. There in the silence kneel Mary and Joseph and the shepherds, as though waiting. And I hear somewhere in the recesses of my sleepy mind the words of Wisdom: "When peaceful silence lay over all, and night had run the half of her swift course, down from the heavens, from the royal throne leapt your all-powerful Word ..."

As I go out into the night I find myself wondering if that text is what makes us assume that Jesus was born in the middle of the night. I was racking my brains for any evidence in the Gospel, other than the circumstantial, that the birth took place at night time.

I suppose the presence of the star lends weight to it, but the star did not necessarily appear at the moment he was born, did it? Likewise, though the shepherds hear the news keeping watch by night, there is no real reason to assume that this is simultaneous with the birth.

In that strange alertness induced by the emergency call and the frosty night air and the anticipation of what I am going to find at the hospital, suddenly I feel the reason. I feel the ebb-tide of human activity; the strange amplified silence of the dark, and the ineluctable reality of death abroad in the loneliness of the night hours.

Theologically we know he was born in the dead of night. At the midnight of the darkest time of the year the light appears. The darkness symbolises human frailty and fear – all that is sinful and occult pressing down on the world.

The Grace of God is most active and potent at the precise point where human power and human meriting are weakest, most needy. So the terror of the night is tamed by the child who brings the light of heaven on the midnight.

As I return from the hospital there are the silhouettes of Mary and Joseph in the quiet house, waiting still, a sign of the infinite and only comfort and hope in the night for the man who has just died in the hospital – and for me, struggling to minister to him. "Wake up, O Man!" cries St Augustine in a Christmas sermon. "It was for you that God was made man! Awake sleeper, and arise from the dead and Christ shall give you light."

Those I serve are serving me

Christmas Day seems a very long time ago; it is only nine days as I write. There were two Christmasses this year, I felt: a parish one and a hospital one. The parish one was, as it were, what I knew to expect from previous years, but it was very special and lovely to be in my own parish. I suppose a parish is like a family, in that the way you celebrate Christmas brings to the fore all that is loving and holy, as well as sometimes throwing into relief what needs to change, or what has been lost. There was, for me at least, a sense of peace in the parish and a sense of rediscovering the gifts and the value that are there, but which from week to week we can take for granted.

Providence was bountiful too. God sent me an angel in the form of a new sacristan, actually a nurse at the hospital. A week before Christmas she took over the sacristy and worked for hours and hours reorganising, cleaning and sorting it out. She washed the linen, cleaned the plate, turned out the drawers and totally transformed the place so that it gleams. All is calm, all is bright, all shines to the glory of God.

I was concerned that I would have no organist. Our regular organist had already warned me that his family go away at Christmas so he was unable to come. At the last moment two of the music staff from the Catholic secondary school volunteered and one played for Midnight Mass and one on Christmas morning, and we had sweet music and really joyful singing. The church looked magnificent; the new crib is quite splendid, and we had a packed church. Even on Boxing Day both Masses were full, which, I must confess, pleasantly surprised me.

The hospital was peaceful on Christmas Day. There was a quiet calm about it as I went in with Communion and the people I saw seemed to be very accepting of their lot. It remained quiet until the afternoon of Boxing Day; in the days that followed I attended many deaths and many crises.

In the midst of this, there has been a little oasis of peace and tranquillity each day. There is a priest in the hospital, a dear man who is retired and lives outside the diocese, continuing to supply, even apparently in my parish, though before my time. When I first visited him he told me that when he was first ordained he was sent to a parish which had five hospitals and, in his own words, he would run around "like a scalded cat". His gratitude for my visits means a lot, coming as it does from someone who understands what the work is like. I have experienced anew that paradoxical and humbling phenomenon of being ministered to by those to whom you think you are ministering.

On Christmas Day I heard his confession, anointed him and gave him Communion, and so at the coming of the Word made flesh we celebrated together these transforming sacraments which continue to mediate the Divine Word among our human nature. The priest's reverence, the reverence of a lifetime's service recalled me from scalded-cat mode and showed me the possibility that this can give way to deep surrender and peace. So habituated was he to anointing other people, that when the time came he forgot to turn his hands over (you anoint a priest on the back of his hands because he has already had the palms of his hands anointed with chrism at ordination). He communicated a deep and serene faith, and from his hospital bed he taught me that truth we all need to learn over and over again: that priesthood is not an occupation, what someone does, but what someone is, or is becoming, by co-operating with God's grace. It is not that I turn my hands to the task, rather I place them into another's hands.

Each day we chat a little; he feels very deeply the disaster in South-East Asia and hopes that it will turn men's minds to the frailty of man. Often we outdo one another in putting the Church to rights. He has some great stories to tell from his long priestly life. As the days go on he is understandably frustrated by a lack of news or progress in his own case. The holidays have meant that he is in the medical equivalent of a holding pattern. The ward fills and empties around him. On Christmas Day he was all alone in a bay of six beds, but he still managed to give me the impression of a resigned peace, passing the day with his breviary and his rosary and reading *Communio*.

The relative quiet of the holidays has also allowed some lovely encounters with staff: chats with poor overworked doctors who are glad just to be able to let off steam; a young porter who stops me and asks if I will hear his confession.

It's not a Christmas I could have planned or envisaged, but one richer in blessings for that, I am sure.

Lightning Source UK Ltd.
Milton Keynes UK
UKOW04f0726071217
313975UK00001B/2/P